REFUGIUM

Caitlin Press Inc.
8100 Alderwood Road,
Halfmoon Bay, B.C. V0N 1Y1
www.caitlin-press.com

Text and cover typeset by Vici Johnstone
Cover art and design by Sharon Montgomery
Printed in Canada

Caitlin Press Inc. acknowledges financial support from the Government of Canada and the Canada Council for the Arts, and the Province of British Columbia through the British Columbia Arts Council and the Book Publisher's Tax Credit.

Library and Archives Canada Cataloguing in Publication

Refugium : poems for the Pacific / Yvonne Blomer, editor.

ISBN 978-1-987915-53-2 (softcover)

1. Pacific Ocean — Poetry. 2. Pacific Area — Poetry. 3. Canadian poetry (English) — 21st century. 4. American poetry — 21st century.

I. Blomer, Yvonne, editor II. Title: Poems for the Pacific.

PS8287.P33R44 2017   C811.008'09164   C2017-904600-4

Refugium

Poems for the Pacific

EDITED BY
Yvonne Blomer

Caitlin Press

for Colwyn

and for the tiniest sea creature that we have neither seen
nor perceived, but who lives, must live.

CONTENTS

re·fu·gi·um
an area in which a population of organisms can survive
through a period of unfavourable conditions,
especially glaciation

The sea is everything. It covers seven tenths of the globe...
The sea is only a receptacle for all the prodigious, supernatural things that exist
inside it. It is only movement and love; it is the living infinite.

— *Twenty Thousand Leagues Under the Sea*, Jules Verne

REFUGIUM:
A CONVERSATION ON GRIEF AND THE SOLACE OF POETRY

In recent centuries the universities have supported an exploitation of the Earth by their teaching in the various professions, in the sciences, in engineering, law, education, economics. Only in literature, poetry, music, art and occasionally in religion and biological sciences, has the natural world received the care that it deserves.

— Thomas Berry in his introduction to *The Great Work*

At the age of twelve, I became a lacto-pesco vegetarian, and at eighteen stopped eating fish the instant I saw a swordfish caught during a snorkeling trip off Maui. I had just been swimming with gorgeous, sparkling, colourful fish and now one hung by a hook off the back of the ship. I felt isolated in my shock, isolated in my belief that what I had witnessed was wrong, that to swim with this creature and then kill it and hang it from the boat was wrong. I couldn't reconcile the sport of fishing with how I felt. For centuries we have fished and over-fished, and we have thrown our waste and our losses, griefs and wishes into the Pacific Ocean. It has offered us refuge as we mourn, and now I hope we can begin to offer it a similar chance to heal.

As the city of Victoria's poet laureate, I decided with my application that I would use my position to do something to draw attention to the plight of the Pacific Ocean. Rising ocean temperatures are killing coral reefs, cities dump raw sewage and factories raw waste into it, densovirus is killing sea stars, and seabird populations are falling. The amount of plastic in the ocean continues to grow and the acidification of the ocean continues to increase as its temperature rises. My hope is that the poems in *Refugium* will create conversations, that they will be a *refugium* to the reader and perhaps to the Pacific and her creatures.

In a recent paper titled "New Sadness," Tim Lilburn writes that the kind of climate change that is occurring now, enacted through our activities on the earth, will create a sadness we will not know how to live within. He writes, "It is likely the interiority appropriate to a catastrophe of such magnitude does not lie within the bounds of our current imagination." Lilburn notes that scientists are as traumatized by their research as artists and writers, but fear showing bias, while poets, on the other hand, are wary of appearing overtly political, lecturing and didactic. Perhaps they are also wary of losing the lyric or metaphoric language integral to poetry.

Though the consequences of becoming political in art are considerable, the consequences of remaining silent out of fear are far more grievous. We must write poems and enter the deep sadness in which we are living. We must sit close to the things that are dying and bear witness. We must continue to have conversations and to make those conversations public.

After attending several presentations and panels on poetry and the environment over the last several months, I find myself often disturbed, listless and despairing. Grief manifests itself in very real ways. In the throes of my own grief, I have turned to completing this book. I have turned to the poems here. I turn to them to deepen and embrace the grief, to remember the deep connection I feel to the ocean and to give shape and specificity to my panic. I also turn to the Pacific by walking along it, standing at its tideline, dipping my foot in and cycling along its shores.

I turn to Tim Bowling's "Found Poem of Strait of Georgia Insults" and imagine the ocean saying to me, "you lungworm you screwshell," and I embrace the insult. I turn to John Barton's poem, "Alexander Mackenzie Reaches the Pacific," and experience that pinch of loss and astonishment at the notion of a time before logging and driftwood-covered beaches. I hold my breath for Heidi Greco's second chance. The poems are doing what I hoped they would do: they are creating a *refugium* — an area in which a population of organisms can survive through a period of unfavourable conditions. We are the organisms; we have created the unfavourable conditions, and we must not only take refuge, but enter our deepest places to witness and take action.

I'd like every reader to refuse plastic bags and straws, to buy drinks in reused glass or tin, and to think before buying or throwing something away. I'd like us to consider what we eat, how we get around, what we wear and where it comes from, what we use and where it will end up.

I am a poet, not a scientist. I am an idealist, too, and hopeful that each small thing we do will make some difference. Think how quickly we changed from aerosol cans when we learned the ozone was seriously depleted. I am hopeful, and I am in despair. Today, July 25, 2017, the Pacific NorthWest LNG project to build a gas liquefication and export facility on Lelu Island in Port Edward, B.C., has been cancelled. We can make changes; just as we have moved from the industrial revolution to the consumer and computer age, we can adopt new and different ways of living, ways that are beyond what we have imagined up to now, ways of living that protect with respect and equality the planet and her creatures. We can stop the refusal Jan Zwicky speaks of in her poem "Seeing": "Even now, even now, / to fail to give thanks: the same/ lethal refusal, same/turning away from the beauty/that is."

I'd like you to think of this book as a hand held out to you, inviting you into a conversation that is one part of a larger conversation, perhaps the most important one to take place in our Anthropocene age.

Yvonne Blomer
July 25, 2017, Victoria, B.C.

CONNECTION: THE PACIFIC AS PART OF OUR FAMILY

The rugged coastline, where North America ends and the Pacific Ocean begins, captures our imagination. No matter how long you have been here, one month, one year or a thousand, the Pacific is part of the family.

We welcome a new member of the J-Pod Orca clan, as if she were our daughter, our sister or our niece, the sockeye count is a measure of our success and failure and the trade winds swirl controversy from the Juan de Fuca Strait to the Inside and Douglas Channels.

The issues that come and go with each new tide, churn emotions captured by the lens, the brush, and the poet's pen. These are stories to be shared with our little ones, who are born with salt in their veins.

TheWSÁNEĆ (Saanich) and the KELLOLEMEĆEN (Orca) are cousins who fish together and when their SĆÁÁNEW_ (salmon) relatives return to earth each year making good on an ancient contract, the ultimate selfless sacrifice. Do we honour our part?

The Pacific is a place of extremes, reflecting the best and the worst we see. The Pacific is where we work, play, celebrate, and where we grieve.

The Pacific tests us, challenges us, pushing us to the limits of our fear and greed. The Pacific rewards us, replenishing our bellies, our inspiration, our spirit, reprieve.

Amidst uncertainty, we seek the Pacific, *pācificus*, the peace within our family, to renew relations and secure our home. We seek to even our scale pans and recognize our side of the deal. Moderation and self-control.

We are all explorers, exploiting the Pacific for her bounty. How do you capture the energy in the forests and along the beaches? Enjoy this collection of experiences. They are family stories, some old, some new, inspired by our home and the power of the Pacific.

Adam Olsen
WJOLELP (Tsartlip), WSÁNEĆ (Saanich Territory)
MLA, Saanich North & the Islands

What We Heard about the Sea

by Rachel Rose

Once we belonged. We belonged for wet
millenniums, then we exiled ourselves

gill by gill, fin by fin. The sea sang us forth,
first birth, first Eden,

our blood tide brackish. The Fall
was a struggle to shore, sip of sharp air.

We can't even name how we long to go home,
but still that desire

swims in us. We return to visit
with buoyancy compensators, masks

and tanks of air, we sink
and look and remember

how it felt to live here,
but we are tourists now. Cold gold

light in water, we touch the brittle fingers
of black coral, feathered tongues of barnacles,

even the great wings of manta rays
that swoop over us

and we suck hungrily
on our mouthpieces

swallowing back our salt, yearning
for the time we lived here

when we could fly.

WHAT THE SEA PERHAPS HEARD

by Rachel Rose

Killer whales hunt a blue whale calf
and eat his tongue. As he bleeds to death,

blood seeps without a sound into my body.
The gulls come, screaming their belly-greed,

the small fish come with their needle teeth.
The mother blue has more grief

in her massive body
than anything else I have held.

No one has seen what I see: how the great white sharks
copulate, fitting together in secret method.

And when the octopus siphons me inside her,
and I unfurl her delicate legs with warm currents,

she blushes for me alone. I hold the tight curl
of the seahorse's tail as he pivots,

protecting his basketful of life.
Observe the spaghettini arms of starfish

reaching for drifting food. Hear their little song:
the stomach, the stomach! Dear urchins, sweet limpets.

All feast in me. In the heat of my armpit
waves curl their black seaweed, stones groan

as they are ground to sand. I rock them.
In my cold brain I am rational,

I do not weep to feel the polar bears
scrape my frozen cheeks.

I do not weep when the belugas
sing or narwhales leap like unicorns

and when icebergs collapse I am
scraping dead skin from my forehead

so I can think better, that thunderous, cleansing
crash. Sometimes I catch your broken boats

and your broken bodies, your diamond necklaces,
your New World apple trees, I accept everything,

I turn no one away. That's me gripping your line, your net,
your boots in invitation, dragging your thighs as you run.

At dawn the grey whale fills his baleen
with a noise like water falling through feathers

and at dusk you sail your boats
across my belly, dragging your hands

as you stare into the wet green silk, like a child looks
under his mother's dress

thinking she won't notice, to see
where he came from.

Reflections

re·flect
to turn into or away from a course
to bend or fold back
to think seriously about

"Posted like silent sentinels all around the town, stand thousands upon thousands of mortal men fixed in ocean reveries."

"...this mysterious, divine Pacific zones the world's whole bulk about; makes all coasts one bay to it; seems the tide-beating heart of earth."

— *Moby Dick* by Herman Melville

Found Poem of Strait of Georgia Insults

by Tim Bowling

You're a Dull Oregon grape you black-bellied plover of a long-billed dowitcher. You lugworm you screwshell. What a walleye pollock of a Kelp-encrusting Bryozoan. Yeah, you heard me, you Suborbicular kellyclam Twelve-tentacled parasitic anemone. Your scaup's always been Lesser you three-spine stickleback Spring-headed sea squirt. That's right, you Hairy chiton, I said it. Don't give me any of your Green falsejingle, you Fat gaper. Who do you think you are, the Lord dwarf-venus himself? You're nothing but a Flap-tip piddock with an Aggregated nipple sponge. Come on, you Pile worm you Dubious dorid you squat lobster. You want a piece of me? Agh, you're all Hollow green nori you yellowleg pandalid. I wouldn't waste my time on a solitary tunicate like you. Yeah, so's your mother you Oblique yoldia. Goddamned mud shrimp. Surf scoter. Seaclown triopha. Gribble. Sea noodle. Dunce cap limpet. Bladderclam. Whelk.

Verses, the Ocean, the Tipping Point

by Arleen Paré

Found poem from internet article

Collapsing dead areas now reported
in the Pacific   dead dead or metaphorical dead
vs protecting 30 percent   they say
the recovery benefits
benefit the whole ocean
vs   days of real anguish   real tears
and despite massive inaction   the unknowing
is massive   this week could decide collapse vs
conservation   they say   oceans
cover 71 percent of the world
this planet   so much is deep water   so much is salt
home to thousands
species we have not yet discovered
sustaining all life   all the time
life on this earth
the World Conservation Congress wonders how
to save
oceans   vs fishing lobbies   vs greed vs
climate change vs pollution
cruiseships   plastic bags   oil spills
birds dying in black rainbow slicks vs
saline solutions
vs massive public campaigning vis a vis
the internet   vis a vis
click here to save our oceans
vs incomplete   massive public apathy vs
facebook   vs instagram   vs two glasses of wine
verses
words   massive   public and personal
collapse   material or psychic   oceans
us   in complete overwhelm

MURALS

by Patricia Young

At Long Beach I sit in a plastic lawn chair,
facing the ocean, binoculars raised. I am looking
for a whale. I would like to tell my children
how its gigantic body leapt out of the waves,
graceful as a minnow. How it slid,
a shimmering blade back into the foam.

I don't know that sitting at the edge
of the Pacific I am more likely to see an elephant
tap dance on water.

There is much I don't know —
that the last whales mutated, their flippers transforming
into wings. That they churned and flapped their tails
until their thunderous bodies rose into the air.

They flew toward the cities. Up and down the coast
they swam into the sides of tall buildings:
hospitals, banks, insurance companies.
Spread themselves across the blank
canvases on every street corner.

A storm whips across the bay.
I have been sitting so long and I am cold,
please someone, tell me to go home, tell me
they are happy up there, pressed like colossal
blue butterflies against cement walls.

ALEXANDER MACKENZIE REACHES THE PACIFIC

by John Barton

Near Bella Coola, July 22, 1793

The beaches bore no driftwood, the old growth
Fell in storms, was felled for totems, no cut
Logs sprung loose from booms drivers later butt
Down stream, salmon hatchlings sped by the flow

From discrete river mouths to flit through silt
From high inland this side of a divide
The land could never feel, the split belied
By fresh water parting north and west, guilt

Nothing he thought of looking for a route
To China, the first Englander to cross
A margin we've breached deeper since with lost
Bearings in good conscience he'd not dispute

Not knowing how far they'd shift as he plied
Through salt, the flights of salmon thousands wide.

ORIGINS

by Bruce Rice

Where nothing is, small desires
have consequence.

In our night harbour, the indifference of the ocean is benign. Its slender breath
pushes us to shore for hours, like love, we imagine.

The colour of every inlet is different yet water cupped in the hand
is transparent. Memory is like this.

A child knows our home is a starfish, dangling its arm
in the millennial tide. Further out nebulae curl crimson as tubeworms,

a shy luminescence: *Which abyss did we come from?*
Riding a planet-size rock. Yahoo.

~

When we hunt we must travel. Therefore remember.
To forget is to die. Every bay has an echo so name it.

These islands move, evolving into themselves, a dictum on survival —
seeds in a mudball, and millions of lives in trust of the feet of birds.

The most natural thing is to want to know
where weather comes from,

the ways beaches differ —
ropy and treacherous, or a midden of shells,

a place to inhabit a week or a season, the sea's floating skin
measured in microns on which we sail.

EDGY

by Heidi Greco

the end of isolation, the beginning of understanding. — Unknown

Here at the shoreline, a world
begins:

waves lapping,
liminal

granting a second
chance.

ATKINSON LIGHT

By Gary Geddes

Your going that way.

I admit I was curious,
empty boat nudging the rocks
at Point Atkinson, motor running.

A brief notice in the *Daily Province*,
the usual flutter of relatives,
embarrassed by the open-endedness
of the affair.

~

Peter, the old man said,
Peter that went to Canada.

A crumbling harbour, a dozen
grey stone houses, holding back
the North Sea. I stand
at the mouth of the Spey River

and understand your leaving.

Tenacious Scots, never far
from laughter and despair, clinging
to the shore like barnacles.
A nation of exiles, one foot
always in water.

The river empties,
speaks volumes.

~

Water baffles us.

Contained, it can be measured,
given shape and colour, harnessed
to cut rock, illuminate cities.

Lacking form, it calls
to things inside we'd thought
forgotten.

~

A bright day, sun glinting
off North Shore windows, parkside firs
reflected in coal black water.

Someone stirs slightly
as you step across the moorings
to your boat, hears
the slow reluctant firing
of the engine. Two early gulls
make low sweeps over the wheelhouse,
settle to rest on pilings.

A door opens on the Texaco
marine station in Coal Harbour.
Attendant emerges, yawns,
watches you round the point,
make toward the Narrows.

~

You choose an element
that, having none, distorts
the shape of things.

From my room at college
I could see the Atkinson Light,
its single eye scanning
the broad reaches of the bay.

Locked in my green imaginings,
I'd see you on the waves,
a dead man holding the living
on his knee.

And Charley McCarthy me,
feeling my lips move
silently.

~

Bucking the current, a strong westerly,
almost an hour clearing the bridge.
High on sunshine and Scots whiskey,
you cut the engine, drop a line

over the side.

What's in a name?

The *ged*, in Geddes, the pike
a scavenger, bottom
feeder.

~

Port Gordon to the port
of Vancouver, from womb
to oceanic womb.

Time does not matter,
forever getting there, the long
slow crawl over the land.

~

How to survive, believable,
the selective memory
of relatives?

Water batters the seawall.
I gather a few shells, burrow
among smooth stones.

~

Become the bottle
you are holding, drift seaward
containing a cryptic message.

I take my soundings.

Your empty boat nudges
my mind, lean pike
stares from my eyes,

Atkinson Light makes its
slow revolutions.

How I Envy Jellyfish

by Rebekah Rempel

I envy their malleability. Boneless,
they take any form they wish: ghosts
in shimmering gowns, hoar-frosted willows,
orchards of glowing fruit. They are the ocean's cumulus clouds,
the blue whale's dreams, ancient gods'
eyes that have seen eternity.

I envy their wisdom. With crystalline tongues
they drink the sea's subconscious, tasting
each kind of darkness. They know
the current better than the water itself, remember
the womb better than we do.

I envy their immunity. They have no use for the sun or moon
to guide their way, clutching light inside them
like the breath they'll never need to take.
And in all their isolation, they don't feel
loneliness, always gathering together.

How I envy their grace as they bell through their lives
tolling silence. I envy their release, their unabashed
weeping. The way they enter the deepest abyss
and rise back up, unscathed.

Pacific Variations

by Stephen Collis

1.

Like a grey glass
open book
vase of wildflowers
wallpaper chair and
peaches in a bowl
the joy of light as
the background
disappears
and the forest for its
trees is released
oceanward
from the frame

2.

What was clear
cut was the fish
the camera the dear
dead at the side
of the coast road the
water rocks and
humpbacks
running cross panel
to interrupt the hunt
nature no mort
the incidence
of this astounding
a gull's weight
in new ideas
things lost over
the ocean and
found again and
who said altruism
who said rescue?

3.

I hardly lift my pen to move
outside the light is not
not receding it is
a hawk's wing a turn
in another direction
the line the pen can hardly
not follow its flight
to the west of here
to what remains a
shell on a Pacific beach on
the brink of elsewhere
a shell on the path
on the brink of the park
a shell dropped in midden
next to the ear of a shell
still listening to birds not
not coming back anymore

WOLF

by Patrick Lane

Wolf prints on the estuary and the long, slow mutter
where water breaks on sand, the broken crystals,
stone reduced to the myriad confusions we call chaos
that comes clear only when we reduce it to the few,
an eye staring into a hand that once was mountain, sand,
thin shells, and stone. And the wolf who passed through
in the night, his paws leaving a steady track, stopped
here and played a moment with a bit of driftwood
in the tidal wrack. I read the simple signs,
where he turned and leaped and turned again
like any animal in love with the dawn, his belly
full of a deer he brought down in the ferns by the creek
beyond the stand of firs and cedars. Then to play.
A solitary animal, no other tracks beyond the early
claws of crows and ravens. On a tidal stone a heron
stares down into his beard. Hunched shoulders, long beak,
he waits for salmon fry in the diminishing waters. Once,
I came here with a woman and we lay in the heat of the day.
As the sun fell away she ran naked across the sand,
the sweat of her love drying on her small shoulders.
I chased her until we fell laughing on the same line of shore,
her hands and mine and the curve of her thigh at rest.
Years ago now. Here is where the wolf played
and here is where his paws turned the sand
as he turned back to the swordfern and the cedars.
I am sure it was here. That line of hills and that fir
leaning out over the waters. I am sure the tree is the same tree,
the broken crown where an eagle rested, that one branch
where the kingfisher fell into the shallows years ago.

MAN-MADE

by Terri Brandmueller

On the beach
a smooth spruce pole
loosed from its boom
nudged the shore's tangle
of rusted cable and twisted gill net,
mussel-crusted pylons and polystyrene
wrack,
teredo-eaten railway ties and the sharp
black carcass of an outboard motor, but
we couldn't find the sand —
not in the glacier-scoured inlets or
on the tidal flats of Wickaninnish
not past weedy rocks,
or even free blowing on rock-hard sand bars.
The only sand was in the glass fish float from Japan,
a giant green eye, sea-worn
from years in the
north Pacific
drift,
and
winking
in the wash

PASSAGE: FJORDS & ISLANDS

by Jeremy Pataky

Tides noticeably stretch the oceans, and to a small extent, the solid mass of the planet. The earth and its oceans are continuously deformed by the tides of the moon and sun, suffering, in effect, a frictional loss of kinetic energy. The earth's rotation is slowing — over 100 million years the day will increase by an hour.

1.

Another sundown, a bit more ease:
holes blossom in fold junctions of charts.
Off a beach once emptied by smallpox,
we gather oysters. A steam donkey
is skewered by a hemlock.
Dogwood onshore, salmonberry, bears,
hummingbird, and salal.
Shell bits in the bilge like a mess of otoliths.
Archaic seas clarify the day's matted hue.
Land of feathered water,
cedar-anchored mussel colonies, bipinnate
salt stain and wind. Forget limpets,
chitons, herons, and sandhill cranes.
Forget bentwood boxes, goose barnacles, pink
scallops and broken cockles,
beach-bleached, cast up on history's wet ruins.
Forget cormorants and scoters,
unlearn fish weir and kayak. "I say we turn the whole damn
island into a stump farm." Go without legend, go silent.
Your accidental breath, these unfortunate lungs,
a gill-glyphed neck chapped by wind.

2.

Tide residue, middens.
Defunct cannery, an old potlatch island.

In a room like a sinus cave
a woodsplit measle-house breathes brine effluvium.
How many tongues were removed on this rock?

Holy lichen, sunk ship, deer gutpile.
No place without coordinates.
Ruins more soil than relic —
the water kills and sustains.

3.

The water kills and sustains:
bays float forests that once reflected.
Mosquito-bother. Floatplane buzz.
Where moss absorbs all manners of speech
a raven rails jeremiads into hemlocks.
Old rope powder coats these calloused hands.

4.

These moments were days' bones.
We clutched a course with compass
and tiller, forgot south. Used the word line
for ropes that reined wind.

Whole faces, tastes, all that we'd forgotten
coagulated, string-wise,
in the brainwork of our hands.

We immersed so much: lures and crab pots,
anchors and coffee grounds, sunglasses,
orange peels, cutlery, fish carcasses
and the corners of sails, crab carapaces,
our arms to elbows as we groped tide wind,
sky of kelp forest and all its fin-winged inhabitants.
Let us remain here. Let us remain still.

Tethered

by Linda Crosfield

Puffer fish litter the low-tide sand.
Frigate birds float above the sea,
fairweather kites tethered to Earth
by strings of hunger
held taut by fish they seek.
One circles, dives,
comes up with silver in its mouth.
Small change for a hungry bird
working the cavernous sea.

RESIDUAL

by Anita Lahey

Every tide this brilliant toss
reassembles. Fish head. Crab carcass.
Gulls call carnage. Seaweeds
drape beach grit and barnacles
spent and glowing:

sloshed violin strings,
gutted accordions, a sea serpent's
outrageous sperm. Trace the glistening
container ships, packed
solid, serenely floating —
The dignity

these mist-shrouded
ships convey, the calm
that deflects Poseidon's scorn,
defies the trinkets tucked
among their stores. I turn
my eye to the crows, I live

among them now, the original
beachcombers, poking and sifting,
discarding a clam shell here,
skirting a puddled jellyfish
there, the whole arrangement

sprinkled with plastic chips
sunnier than a yellowlegs' legs,
more profanely orange than
the oystercatcher's bill,
residue so arresting

it's inspired art. Mornings,
evenings, here they come, tide out,
tide in, by wing, by foot, these
spry devils, snickering
and scheming.

BROWN TURBAN SNAIL

by Gillian Wigmore

brown turban snail
jewelled top snail
secret in the bull kelp fronds
at the start of the dark
snails on jellied safety
on dinner
on filtered sunlight

brown turban snail
jewelled top snail
shyshark, gumboot chiton
what noise? what uncertain
certainty: the slick thickness
of ribbons, green and gold
and bending, waving
thick whips of stalk disappearing
downward

brown turban snail
jewelled top
agitated at the edge
of above and below
neighbours with melibe, garibaldi
oh snail, oh shyshark
march of eat and ocean of day
night and day, the wash of sky
through the grass-green sea

brown turban snail
jewelled top snail
cabazon, kelpfish, hush
washed just underwater
ponderous
slow wander on the kelp fronds
rasp the film of diatoms
with your filelike tongue

COMPARATIVE BIOLOGY

by Jamella Hagen

Skirting the wet west edge of Yakobi Island,
I thread a kayak through foamy ocean synapses,
trace the hesitant tip of a compass needle
toward a wave-whipped lace of rock
in the fog. Overhead, the man in the helicopter
radios us a go-ahead. *Check the back cove,*
the famous whale biologist is filling her crates.
We spill onto the pebbled beach, find her
in hip waders, combing the shoreline
with a briny armful of bones. She sends us
to the far beach, where Laura and I pull orca vertebrae
from a tangled mass of seagrass.
We hold them for a photograph, a lesson
in comparatives: the orca vertebrae
as large as our heads, the two of us
posed before the wide mouth
of the Pacific, behind us a blurred shape
over the horizon, as of clouds or even
the distant towers of Tokyo
bent around the curve of the earth by light.

Ocean Child

by Terry Ann Carter

for Sophie Valentina, six months in utero

Watching light move over the mountain
I write your name in sand believing

the brief gasp of not-yet lungs
will transform into breath.

I imagine you, little papaya,
riding the embryonic tide. The slight

nudge of you. I wonder what is knitting
together, the pleasure of unfurled ferns

your small spine a crustacean in freefall.
Your throat still too weak to speak of what

is written on water: the whorled promises,
your four-ventricled heart, the colour of your hair.

In sleep and dream what slips through
your fingers: something resembling love.

Awake in the dark I sense your stillness
like a moon jelly at rest on the moonlit sea.

THE WEST STRANGLED SEA

by Makyla Curtis

me te reo Māori / with the Māori language

I hear you whisper a raw journey above
the west strangled sea;
keep coming river
with voices tumbling: come down,
slip down the slick leaves
that drip and drip, a spate of
arching utterances that push.

My ribbon breath coalesces in the air
the west cracks measuring creaking text
breath drip breath:
an air chorus.　　　　　　Your feet, small and huddled
penguin-like — wet legs in the harbour —
a kicking push at the blue tidal ridge.

She is unreadable here;
curling and huddled
uncoiled and reforming the curve of
feet　　　　　　dance tomorrow your words echo 'n
froth along the river, leaving sea foam
bubbling in their wake

moving　　　　cracks closed and curled
but grasping edges clamp, caress, so tightly
— the crevice is a small highway　　　　a highway nuzzling tall
crude soot slushing against the shore
rhythmic and muck, muck black wick alight
a bitter track　　　　　me haere atu　　　　　me haere atu.

Already autumn,   a surf of honeycomb fractures
fractures the light   coarse grit
black stoned beach.
Her breath is calm, the shore line undulating,   rising
a rolling lull as she moves.   In your throat

the slim scale rubs
against hills of text, rubbing the sky down
toi toi fingers pluck   and   feather   along the ribbon road
that curls those wheels around
our mountains, our hulk,

giants against the sea, raw at the stories, raw at the storm
a solitary tree between air lit lights
our follicles prickle at the dust   the three of us
a sluggish dawn where the sun rises
my tongue is ash dried and drying.

Pīhia āku kōmuhumuhu.
the pattern — thrashing in the surf:
the dark centre of a voice.

Me haere atu — go away (polite imperative)
Toi toi — cabbage tree
Pīhia āku kōmuhumuhu — pay no attention to my ramblings / murmuring.

THE YOUNG RAVENS THAT CRY

by Russell Thornton

The trees here twist the ocean up through the night of their roots —
the ocean burns away out of their arms into the day.
The raven rides the repeating croak and call

of its shining-eyed need and demand. The animal that hates
carries his old expulsion as far as he can,
and arrives at a new paradise. His God loves him

even when he lays down pipelines, launches tankers,
exudes sadness and shame. His God keeps in sight
the huddled fledglings, touches the slenderest hair,

while the raven turns its young early out of its high nest,
and the young call for food from a mother that does not exist,
vanished into the blackness of their wings.

The raven's other call, a rainforest's soft, rhythmic bell,
Elijah heard when the flock fed him near a brook.
Tales retell themselves like returning waves —

here tiny-skulled shore birds wander bitumen-slicked.
The heirs of eternity eat royal food, cry
thinking the Holy Spirit is speaking in them. Unclean

flesh, blood, bone and black feathers, the raven
tries to see everything on the shore, scavenges, cries alone.
The raven that flew off with the ball of light

that it found hidden in black box within black box
tears open a bewildered black shore bird,
picks through to the heart and finds food. The animal

that hates looks out over the ocean at the sun
and sees into the black boxes of his heart. In the last box
the dark-raying bird of the sun, the God turned out of the nest,

is feasting on him like carrion. He hears no grieving cry
for the gap he makes in the creation or for the shore
beautiful as at its first sunrise when he darkens it.

MOON JELLY

by Nancy Pagh

for Sallie Tisdale, diving

No stars or moon in sooty sky;
rain falls through cedars
in the mouth
of Jorsted Creek.

My flashlight catches startled crabs
the open
hungry anemones
beside me in this water now.

I am embraced by moon jellies —
transparent
made of tissue, or fog
frail as soap bubbles

floating, turning themselves
almost inside-out with each pulse,
collapsing
from the wash of my hand.

Oh, moon jelly:
a name to spread on evening toast
and eat
bite by tiny bite.

INTERFACE

by Christine Smart

Eye to eye with a lion's mane, a red bell, the medusa stage.
I track rock-fish, iridescent in the shadows,
purple starfish, sun stars, feather-gilled nudibranchs.

A moon snail's protruding foot smothers a clam.
A crab scuttles, all legs and pincers flailing,
down the white shelf into the abyss.

The ocean's rhythm, tides and currents, the slosh
and burble. I climb the ladder to the boat,
doff mask and snorkel, fins and suit.

You listen to the weather channel,
check the tide table and chart;
hoist the main, unfurl the jib.

I taste salt and shiver,
head into the wind
close hauled.

Rainier Twice in a Day

by Nicholas Bradley

What next? When I was half the age
I am now, I watched a man pick black-
berries in brambles across the road. Juice
and blood gloved his hands. I would have
said then that the violence and dread
of a time of war purpled his fingers. Or was
it the wealth of a ripe era? Now I revise:
the man, the street, the blackberries
were simply there on Ash Road. I was half my age.

When we took in the Chittenden Locks last
month and strolled along the edge of Shilshole Bay,
eyeballing boats — we'd buy that one someday,
or this one, and be fishers, who are free, or make
a killing in razor clams and Dungeness crabs — omens
were everywhere, like barnacles on dry-docked hulls.
Salt chuck slapped wooden vessels, the concrete breakwater.
Limpets and mussels glistened in shallows.
We caught the last light on the Olympics
across Puget Sound. Unrepentant oysters
delighted in the salty stink while we read stern
names, briny and knotted, on the monument
to the sons of Leif Erikson — Olaf, Dag, Arne,
Einar. *Coho, sockeye, chinook, kokanee,*
chum. Did the magic words bring these Vikings
luck? The odds favoured disaster. Boats
on fire, brothers lost at sea. *Skagit, Tacoma,*
Duwamish: pacific places whisper, beckon.
When the half-moon came out we finished
with Norwegian inscriptions and foraged for dinner
on Ballard's Beemer-fringed streets.

In the morning I watched Mount Rainier
till clouds rolled in. Then clear skies that evening
divulged the volcano — immense, aloof.
I thought of blackberries and the crack of gunshot
when a slab releases to loose an avalanche.
The proximate realm so far from our own
explodes this sphere, remakes it. All the world's
wonders are on display when gates and valves
haul keels up the Ship Canal
while salmon climb the fish ladder. A duet:
alto and *basso*. Everything, Heraclitus said,
is arsy-versy for a time. The ocean
is shipwrecked, and black bear cubs
refuse to descend from trees. I'm neither
mountain nor monument. Your heart
traps mine as summits catch storms. Call
this calm the rain shadow. What will
remain? Zero moves through all things.

TENT ISLAND ANCHORAGE, 1962

by Terence Young

Salt air leaks in
through canvas that is
dew-damp this August morning,
our dying sun drying
pilot-house, foredeck, saloon
top to bottom as it rises
behind sandstone bluffs.

My parents, sister, still sleep,
dream through the insouciant dawn,
deaf to the voice of water
that against our hull
protests its displacement.

Before long, the scent
of late summer maple, then
arbutus bark, broom and fir needles,
a riot in our cockpit shroud,
last night's beach fire, too.

FLATLANDER

by Tanis MacDonald

After Danez Smith

So sister coastline, do you without the slimmest
shred of irony need an aging flatland woman

to point out the ocean's a dudebro god flexing
his glutes at middle-aged humans and laughing at

how we gaze, how we squint into his eventful
horizon? Stop swooning and sighing! It's not good

for him. It makes him think he's all that, a big wet
dick, makes him think he's the trident he rode in on.

Sure, he's got his glorious waves, his majestic
rising tide: no doubt, but stop now and look. See how

he uses the sun like she dawns and sets just for him,
like she's only the light by which he combs his hair?

He sniffs with one nostril, a tic he used to woo
Charybdis and now trots out every chance he gets,

droning on about his pecs with every freshening
breeze. Don't let him convince you that you can never

get enough of his big rollers, his seaweed smack.
Admit it: the Pacific needs to step back and

sit the hell down. The Pacific needs to stop his
strut and grant grief its sodium due, quit boasting

his eternity will wipe us clean. He knows all
too well the high salt content of tears, but he won't

own it. *None of that,* he'll say: *it ruins the mood.*
Grief is for the grasslands under snow who know it

already: tears, fury, rape of a twelve-year-old
salting the fields on Agassiz's lacustrine plain.

SINKING

by Luther Allen

there are those of us
at the bow of the boat
breathing deeply
eyes front
teeth bared
for anything

and those
at the stern watching
what was
disappear with the wake

and the dwindling orcas
who would say
if they could

      there are too many boats
      heedless

      no matter the gaze

Swimming

by Clea Roberts

After you rose at noon,
and I curled your hair,
and you took the pinot grigio
to steady your hands so you could
lift your breakfast spoon to your lips,

we stepped into the ocean together,
me holding your hand
like an injured bird, not out of love
but out of necessity,
the glass surface undulating
in waves up to our shoulders.

I feel so powerful, you said
looking around, and I knew
this was how
I must have felt
when you pulled my infant
body through the water,
the two of us weightless
and in awe.

SEEING

by Jan Zwicky

You've looked now. You've seen.
       The intricate ore,
              the charred sunlight we've bled

to feed our addictions, the seabed
       we've guttered, the soil we've enslaved
              and then raped and then forced

to bear monsters: we've broken
       what's holy. There are no
          other rivers,

no prairies, no air, no clear
       wordless root of the breath.
             No sky but the sky.

Even now, even now,
       to fail to give thanks: the same
             lethal refusal, same

turning away from the beauty
       that is. It's what
             being's made of: light

scoring the dark, dark
       marbling light. You,
             you who are weeping,

look up: it's the sky.
       And the rain that is falling
             is rain.

Humans on It

A dark age comes on little white feet
and every silence we've imagined will be ours.
Sorrow and sorrow and sorrow will be ours.

— Patrick Lane

NOTES ON *WHALE JUMP*

by Méira Cook

The sea is manual today, takes muscle to move.
Humps about like a monster with an itch called Over Here.
In its narrow wooden clogs the catamaran steps
through creaking corridors.

Paint chip colours to press against a mind.
Wine-skin. Candle-burnt-out-fastest. Amnesty-seeker.
Somewhere a whale, whale jumps.
Can't turn around fast enough is the secret
of Whale Jump. Clutching at the day's railing,
mast against, looking out. Like the last frame
in evolution's line drawing. The monkey in us all
finally standing up.

Far away, a whale. Either coming up or going down.
In the distance the pleasure boats come panting
off the long horizon. Trailing jellyfish sonar.
Wherever they've been sea winces to a colour
that is easy to name.

Small Boat: IV

by Kate Braid

> *A gull racking the grey water*
> *screams once, but no one answers.* — E.G. Burrows

i.

I say I won't be afraid, swear
I'll get over this fierce fist to my gut
as the first roller rills under the boat
and I cast off my last tie
to land, leap aboard. I'm playing now —
this is my leisure. Say it again.

I swore I wouldn't be afraid, this time
I'd cast off, *fenders*
(I know the word, took the course)
curl the rope (*line*) carefully, stow it
where I can reach it again, quickly
and (I hope) soon, soon
as we reach the far shore. I swore

I wouldn't be afraid only you didn't tell me
there would be white caps and this upward diving
into a wilderness of water.
I watch you, all your senses poised
(I am brilliant at the details)
knuckles on the boat's wheel, how you tense
into the next wave, bent forward not enjoying
the view, mountains fading.
Black breakers are my foreground now.

Conversation, when there is any,
is a polite fishing around, I stay away
from the terrors of the deep,
go shallow, then

it wasn't a sob just
small breath caught, I couldn't help it as I reached
for my rain jacket, something close and warm
and you noticed, said sharply,
You want to go back.

It wasn't a question.
I forgot courage, forgot promises, everything.
Yes I said, *Yes* and regretted it
too late, remembering it was a promise
too late but grateful anyway

as we headed back to a sliver of bright, silver
hope, to the dock, the blessed shore. But I promise,
I promise, next time....

ii.

Already the sea is lighter, sky clears.
There are no other boats — is this a sign?
Last night I dreamed my favourite gold earring dropped
in the water — is this another?

My heart, small pump, is overcome
by a dark sea of blood and unknown miles
of deep. Something is alive down there.
If I was thrown in the water, how soon
before deathly cold bit?

It doesn't matter how good a swimmer I am
there is nothing here to save me
but a small curved bowl in the ocean,
a thin question mark of gasoline,
and a man's hand on the wheel
dissolving

My Love, the Pacific

by Alana Sayers

I jump in
and listen.
You sing to me
in a lullaby of waves.
Quiet my mind,
silence the fear
so I can hear your words.
Take my body
I trust you.
You hold me
as I float in flowers
where we join
in between our worlds.
You pour water down my back
and turn my heart into rivers

THE SEA IS NOT CELIBATE

by Catherine Greenwood

> *I owe my fine health and long life to the two pearls I have swallowed every morning.*
> — Mikimoto

In the sting of the kelp whip slapping the rocks
and your ebbing desire, a virility potion:
you shrug off my hand and desiccated seahorses
course in a lather through my veins,
the apothecaries' measure of one lukewarm word
weighs a thousand grains of viper blood
stirred with a rare narwhal tusk.

See how the rabbit with pestle and mortar grinds
the culled pearls of the moon?
Her limitless pharmacy dispenses light
to men watching the lovers move
slowly on her rumpled mattress,
the amorous planets in their rut, and below,

the ocean electrified in its own aphrodisiac juice.
Tense as cables the thick eels twitch
in their sockets, clams unclench and open
under the tender strokes of starfish, while tingling anemones
part their soft mouths in purple expectation.

Turn away from me, beloved.
I'm drugged on the crushed pearls of your indifference.

Fata Morgana

by MW Jaeggle

That tanker, the man says,
is carrying progress.

All I see is a mirage, a pregnant
blot gently writhing

in the afternoon sun.
All I see is what it's carrying

pitched across the sea,
this stolen garden, unseeded land.

This progress is ectopic, illusory,
a phantom limb

— arm swimming in a drum,
the rest of the body barrelling down the road —

barrelling
towards global peak,

when black will reach
this beach, my feet,

and paint my toes in
Kafkaesque gore.

Steel amphorae slowly
dances across the ocean's floor.

Paint the Big Island

by Barbara Tramonte

With words

Tell about the walk
To the tide pool
In a way
That screams cadmium
And hala tree flowers
On the path
Past the lookout
To the sea

Tell of your arduous walk
In Japanese fisherman shoes
With felt bottoms
Down a cinder path
Where after the railing ends
You are on your own
Against a terrifying landscape

Come out of the forest
With its snarling undergrowth
Geckos as green as chartreuse

Face the sea

You can't get down to the sea
Until you climb the lava rocks
Some steep, some jagged
A payment for your soles

You grapple;
Up, down
Frantic for footing
While a young bare chested
Man holding a baby in one hand

And a beer bottle in the other
(With a cigarette in his mouth)
Traverses the rocks like they've been
Laid smooth by the
Department of Public Works

You go on all fours
In your skirted bathing suit
While your lovely old sisters
Strike a pose in their hats

Look up

Even if this threatens your footing
You scream inside
At the sight of the tide pool
Waves swell, smash
Coming, coming, coming
A crystalline blue
A Tiffany blue
Before they break
And flood the pool

Find your spot

Grip smooth rocks
Slick with sea moss
They talk to you
As the salt
Seeps into your body

The sun is on your hair

Between you and
The vast Pacific
Just rocks

You are small
You are in a skirted bathing suit
Maybe years go by
Before this impossible sea
Before these volcanic rocks
Before you ever knew anything
It all slips away.

Ocean's Edge

by Melanie Siebert

> *But as long as you remember what you have seen, then nothing is gone. As long as you remember, it is part of this story we have together.*
> — Leslie Marmon Silko, *Ceremony*

I ribboned my untenable forever in wind's forever.

I houred suddenly into nonexistence.

I have wanted to die and now don't want to die.

The silver breach of a massive body flexing
muscle like summer slow jams.

Injury. Strange port tapped into my circulation.

Ocean as sudden and alien as a call from Prince's manager.

Warm body, none of this is given.

Forgive me, sea stars dissolving now, cruelty presses
sometimes even from my love.

One more hour, one more hour,
I called to my mother.

The most beautiful part is the stalling.

Guilty and tender, then unwitnessed
in this velvet, unnamed beginning place.

Spoken into only by what moves everything that moves.

I ribboned too the soft sleeping sounds
of the strangers I have called by name
and signed my name having witnessed

them swallowing the pills to quell the terrifying
voices that come from somewhere.

I consider it part of my job to remember
their solid and tanned child arms and legs
and that sometimes running can be a pure and aimless joy.

Each voice that has put into words wanting
not to live has suffered amid this.
The wallpaper behind the sleeping child's head is an adult projection,
a dreamy biomass bruising knowledge.

Even trusting no one, trusting everything somehow.

Did you too call on the rogue wave that could sweep
your personal inventories into unnamed particles?

The ocean's uninsured collection of shiny musical instruments.

Hard wet sand takes a sky

and puts it under my unsure feet.

Is the dark place something you enter or does it enter you?
I asked the girl who still wished to die.

Unspoken selfhatred, a glacier still laying track.

I gull an insistent current.

One more hour, one more hour,
I call to my mother.

One more hour, one more hour,
I call to the last speakers of a language
that has not been my pharmacy.

Does everyone have a stranger they can talk to about dying?

Moon jellies and their lucky horse shoe gonads
nerving a soft propulsion in the ocean's dented mouth.

Misfires, the ceremonial thoughts I mostly lipgloss.

Brief forms livestreamed from a depth.

I will lift the sky's sheet.

To identify a face.

Guilty and tender, then unwitnessed.

GRACE HARBOUR, DESOLATION SOUND

by Emily Wall

When we wake the next morning
and look over the side to check the anchor:

jellies, jellies, jellies!
The water around us is a thick carpet

of moon jellies, each little orb pulsing,
rising and falling in the tide swell.

Even though we know better, we can't help
stretching out our hands, reaching down.

Who could resist touching the moon,
if it came down, in its thousand little bodies,

and surrounded us? Sometimes we need
to be chosen. Sometimes, we need for belief

to be out of our hands.

THE CLEANER

by Jim Roberts

She has appointed herself the one
who picks up after us. I was down by the tide
and heard, "Hey, got a bag?" Among the logs
she held a cluster of crushed water bottles,
a beer can, tatters of grey sheet plastic.
Yes, I had a bag. "Got two? One for you?"
I did, and we went poking along the seawrack,
hauled out nylon rope twisting into
dark nests of kelp, and bottles, bottles —
we're a culture of containers, it seems —
as more grey tatters pulled out of our fingers.
When we climbed the stairs to the bin, she thanked me.
People smile about people like her:
the strange, who have nothing better to do.

from *Surge* (a long poem)

by Emilia Nielsen

Surge Narrows, the rapids:
Canoe Pass, Beazley, Surge, three narrow rock-laden passages
interlock Maurelle, Read and Quadra Islands,
whitewater pulling towards the ocean floor. Whirlpools
big enough to suck deadheads, whole dinghies,
even the tin-roofed post office shack with the official looking sign:
Surge Narrows, British Columbia, V0P 1W0
rocking wildly in the wake from each passing speedboat.
Big enough to swallow Read General Store's boarded-up windows,
roof painted with seagull shit, salal growing thick,
and the one-room cedar-sided schoolhouse, feral horses cropping
grass to stubble on the school's playing field.

~

During summer drought, deer swam from Maurelle
to Quadra to Read in search of tender grass,
a sinewy shadow following them through the alder.
Golden. The dog whined at night, trailed us
during the day barking, kept us in eyeshot, until a hunter's dogs
treed the cougar by the lake. Forced to shoot, he skinned it,
gave the liver to buddies who asked for it.
Ate until their eyes yellowed.

~

We ate. A crew of us roamed the bay, grubbing
wild things, foraging creek bank, waterfall, estuary:
licorice root ferns stripped from moss and maple tree,
a gummy chew of swamp grass pith, freshwater-filled fronds
popped between tongue and hard palette,
salmonberry shoots peeled from prickly skins
to satisfy our appetite for anything
that tasted of saltwater, earth.

Argument with Captain Vancouver over the Naming of Desolation Sound

by Cynthia Woodman Kerkham

Let's say you had good reason —
take that afternoon in August
I saw a gull swallow a starfish.
Each purple finger sinking
slowly into the sea-bird's bitter sea.
All afternoon I watched
as the Pacific lapped the hull,
sun the sandstone. The gull
agape, anchored in its terrible song,
the sea star taking its little steps
down to ruin.

—

You, Captain, the once-rising star,
slow-swallowed by hierarchy back home,
mad with illness, whipping your way north:
Willm. Wooderson, Seaman: 24 lashes for Insolence;
John Thomas: 36 Lashes for Neglect of Duty.

—

These days I sail to Desolation
with bliss lashing back —
wind flares fabric, clouds
climb the tilting cliffs.

I paddle in coves beneath pictographs:
red ochre fish, ancestors, traps.

—

Reek of rot and sweat rising from your crew
as the Discovery enters the Sound, winds light
and fluky, the everything-dripping of a June drizzle,
serpentine tide — maze of blue islands,
inlets smudged with fir and pine,
blindfolded, you say, *in this labyrinth.*

Lost in your black maze, you launch long boats like water beetles
to survey; turn to astronomy. Trust lunars to show you where you are.

∿

I find my bearings by clouds of moon jellies
afloat beneath my anchored boat,
pulsing the sea's bright night,
their milky way, unfurling.

∿

We can all do it. name from our own sad story.
Desolate you float away
having christened and claimed,
done your duty by King George.
Hold piled with pelts, masks, clubs, and traces
of the nights the crewmen traded
all their pewter plates
for time with the women of the Sound.

What must the women of the Sound have said?

∿

Rolled and stored, your pain-staking charts
still guide me here, and now drunken tankers flock
to navigate these ship-swallowing shores,
threaten to cloak ducks in satin black.

Your lament echoes:

Our residence here was truly forlorn;
an awful silence pervaded the gloomy forests,
whilst animated nature seemed to have deserted.

Perhaps you were a seer, after all.

And who am I? Sheathed in petroleum fleece,
warmed by boat cabin's ticking diesel heat.

～

Power naming: anthropomorphizing
in the age of anthropocene
of acid seas where jellyfish bloom
while their predators vanish.

Moon jellies care nothing for our desolation.
Small bells, illumed by shafts of salty light,
sound in my sternum a deep tuning.

～

In Desolation Sound sage and silver mosses
drip from summer-brown cliffs, pink arbutus
unpeels its skin, evergreens fur the air sweet
and I plunge baptismal into a plush sea.

Some days, rain drums the deck, tumbles through channels,
through veins, beads bright as mercury on the crazed-glass hatch,
slips otter-like overboard,
erodes self to sand, loosens —
kelp ribbon on a breathing wave.

~

I know we have to name,
fumble for direction, descriptors,
some with wounds of history
bruising just beneath

but here, in Desolation, I'll glide with the governing tide
listen to how sea purls sibilant on stone,
names itself, sounds its own.

On Dallas Road

by Isa Milman

Entirely sapphire yesterday's waves.
Up high watched peristalsis, gravity's churn

beneath sandy cliff face, its lemony coat.
Thought "ontogeny recapitulates phylogeny"

a classroom burble from long ago. History of species
written in our code. My limbs replay

the long trek up from darkness,
grief I could not fathom.

I rocked in my cradle in a rickety boat
to refuge on a western shore

yellow broom's perfume —
sorrow's antidote

Glenairley: an Elegy

by David Pimm

Pisaster ochraceus

Life passes in the intertides,
where purple pentacles
once broadcast their spawn —
talisman for a decade
glimpsed between beach huts.
Now I read of viral lesions, wasting,
shed star-arms — wave-washed
mush, gone. As I write, my hand
both amanuensis and echo.

They died
facing west,
the direction of last things —
like England's monasteries,
dissolved.

OUTLIERS OF INDUSTRY

by Lorin Medley

In the ready dusk, fishers purse the net
and drum it aboard; the great feed is underway.
Gulls flock and herring brines the decks — the
remembering salmon will follow;
come the tag days of summer
rivers will dish like copper,
tool up orange-tailed for production
and then the tail and scale of redds to spawn,
end and begin, rot and resurface in bear scat
and nutrient rich soil. Around this staunch industry,
sun rises and sets as drumfire.

Sun rises and sets as drumfire
above pesticides and plastic particles;
it crosses the sky while moon lags behind
and ocean's floor grows faint.
King crabs paw water like the undead;
in rivers, a stunned spawn mourns
the retreat of glacier-fed waters —
earth's climate unspooled.

Beyond the docks, moss-covered rooftops
and leaf-filled gutters,
night wanderings of rat and raccoon,
ditches slick with runoff, asphalt lifted by bamboo
gasping fissures of coal, greenhouse gas emissions
billboards and other contradictions:
big trucks in small spaces,
flooded parking lots, food banks, tent shelters.

Sun rises and sets as drumfire;
offspring of girls who sleep and breathe hockey,
boys you once arm-wrestled or knuckle greeted
have been poached by outliers of industry —
the head-banging, carbon-dioxide-breeding crowd.

WHAT COULD BE MORE ALLURING THAN THE TIDES?

by Beth Kope

we have tabled them and measured neap with moon
cycled and counted. but sit
beside the sea, tell me your eyes
aren't shocked as it slides away so steadily?
just minutes ago that boulder was hidden.
coast grows, sand spreads, rock revealed.
the distance to the water line retreats, retreats.
slick algae sheen, stranded starfish, and kelp beds
scent the air as the sun warms them.
what was the break of a whale's back cresting offshore
is now an island. this is a game of red light
try to catch the moment ocean slackens.
suddenly there is silence.
the shore bends, tide holds before it turns, and then
turns. gulls collide with barnacle-crusted rock and sob.
wing tips slap water. when i look again
the sun has pushed the ocean nearer.

Hook

by Maleea Acker

I miss the grizzled sailors at Telegraph
who smelled of wood smoke, tobacco and rot,
gave us line when ours snagged,
yanked us out when we tumbled from the dock.

I miss the booms, groves filling the sound, ghosts
of toilet paper escaping the through hull, the yellow cloud,
the unbunching turds we scrambled to see. I miss the grey shacks
at Coon Bay while we waited for slack, their white bread, ham fish
hooks, the peeling, beached hulls. A boy my age, lit from within,
ran to the waves, wetsuit askew, alone. I miss
the fires at Montague, the rainstorms we chased to stay
always under the god pelt. Fish condos, docks with red railings,

I miss when the Feds owned everything worth anything on the sea,
prawn boats always full, logs the size of houses, everyone we knew
living aboard or building one in their yard. Then we cursed
out every powerboat on Channel 16, sidled up
to sandstone at Gabriola, nabbed flounder, threw
the same dogfish back cast after cast, his mouth
a bloody mess, still he went
and went for the bait.

I miss the shadowed side of Genoa, water
marine marble — cat's eye
a swirl of orange, someone's old tarp trailing
like a last curtain.

Weather was the first voice: *sea rippled, sea one foot chop* —
it shone doubled with phosphorescent constellations,
oil lamps, alcohol stoves and no regulations
so we floated, mornings, empty Sun Maid
raisin boxes to see if the swans would eat them.
They would. A branch shook on shore
from the left weight of a giant bird

watching summer hook itself in my skin, watching
the last child unencumbered poke his finger
through the net of a crab trap and be punished twice,
once by his father, once by the crab.

Sea amethyst, sea emerald, sea live and jade,
it whirled below the blue-tarped cockpit, under Vega
and the Lyre, a coat we smoothed and dragged and wore —
out of which we could pull, and into which we put,
our shining, unraveling lives.

SHELTER IN PLACE

by Bren Simmers

Timber ship on fire in the harbour.
Phone blowing up with texts.
Breaking news on Global,
stay inside. Wrapped creosote
pilings smudge the sky,
the Tantalus range. All
the newly-laid herring
eggs — dolphins and orcas
lured into Howe Sound
after decades absence —
now a scorched setback.
Upwind, the Chief parking lot
a make-shift drive-in.
Spectators watch twin towers
of smoke, one ashen,
the other coal black.
A Don DeLillo event
in this glaciated valley
where airborne particles
bottleneck. Is this how
it will end? A cloud of dust
or gas or fire, and the TV
telling us not to run,
close your windows,
cover your mouth with a wet cloth.
Hooked to the IV drip
of frontline reportage:
warehouse saved while *crews race*
to stop fire spreading
up the wharf to estuary.
Our fear eighty percent
contained by morning,
they lift the shelter in place

warning. Still no cause.
Terminal VP covers her mouth
with her statement.
The cleanup efforts ongoing.

Tashlik

by Barbara Pelman

traditional ritual on the first day of Rosh Hashona, to cast stones into the sea

Bottom of the hill from Dallas Road,
stone steps that curve around garry oak
and blackberry, broom and bluegrass,
down to a small beach, once a midden.
Selach lanu, forgive us our trespasses.
We are there with the Coast Salish
and with our European ancestors,
our hands full of stones.

Begin here — this stretch of ocean,
flotsam of plastic rings and beer cans
scattered among the driftwood, the carapace of crabs.
Clean the shoreline as you rinse the longing from your hands.
Remember the plastic island the size of Texas
floating in the middle of the bright Pacific.

Sound of the sea, sound of *shofars* blowing
tekiah, teruah, shevarim. A frisson down the spine.
Forgive the knives we have held in our hands,
our upraised arms, fisted. Forgive our words
and our silence. Forgive the paths we are afraid to take,
forgive our wrong directions. I throw my stone,
the one that has sat on my desk all year
collecting the deeds I wish undone,
the ones I should have completed.

Cast your sins upon the water, says the prophet.
Walk along the shore, listen to the rhythm of waves,
the scent of seaweed, the cry of gull and cormorant.
Gather the kelp to feed your gardens —
offer kale, lettuce, squash and zucchini for the hungry
who line up at the food bank, fill the temporary shelters.
The waves thrum like a heartbeat, *tshuvah,* return.
A fist against the heart, *selach lanu.*

selach lanu: forgive us. (from the High Holy Days liturgy)
tekiah, teruah, shevarim: the three different notes of the shofar.
tshuvah: return (also, repent — turning back from wrong directions)

&

by Rob Taylor

a west coast wedding

They weren't prepared for decorations,
speeches, dances, that whole scene.
They'd hardly given thought
to Him, or Her, or the ampersand between —
that antiquated coil
from an outmoded machine
in which they wished to tangle everything,
a knot they'd not been taught, or'd seen.

The fishermen in town, who knew
each hitch and slip they'd need,
now long retired, their boats succumbed
to drydock rot, their holds stripped clean,
the salmon they were purpose-built
to capture now a dream,
the real thing having long since turned
(we tell ourselves tonight) upstream.

from *LOT* (a long poem about growing up on Haida Gwaii)
by Sarah de Leeuw

We are on water.
We land.

We are
on land.

My mother.
My sister.

I step off.
There.

Here.
July 1980.

Another ship.
Always we

are arriving
by ship.

~

Also we have two dogs.
One black, one golden.

The black one is Duma.
The golden one is Tien.

After they die.
We throw both into the Pacific.

I see my
mother sob.

~

About the time.
I begin to develop breasts.

I become obsessed with weight.
The heaviest objects in our house

hold. Our piano. A hide-a-bed. My parents'
king-sized bed. The car, cast-iron pots.

Sometimes my mouth tastes of metal.
After I learn about copper.

Trade and war-canoes made
of single trees, the way cedar floats.

~

Instructions For What You May Not Kill

You may not kill the cedar bark; you may not kill a salmon's skin.
You may not kill a fawn; you may not kill the things that burn.

You may not kill an eel, an otter, or a seal.
You may not kill your foe.

You must never kill your love.
You may not kill a berry on a plant; you must not kill a razor clam.

You must not kill a whale, a snowy mountaintop, a balancing bit
of drop, or even two stray blades of grass on a forest floor.

You must not kill the spot where alders grow.
You must not kill the salt, the water, the tide, or any bits of shore.

You must not kill a cod, a dogfish egg, a baby bird or worst of all her nest.

You may not kill in anger; you may not kill in greed.

You must not kill in spite.
You must not kill a sapling yew.

You must not kill a shrew.
You may not kill a mouse, a mushroom, or the fog.

You must never kill a man
his sister, or his song.

~

Every time we walk.
The dogs.

On the beach.
As a family.

Seals
bark.

THE NEW JERUSALEM

by Joe Zucchiatti

> *Then I saw a new heaven and a new earth for the first heaven and the first earth*
> *were passed away and there was no more sea.* — Revelations 21:1

In the flooring department
at the local hardware store
they sell vinyl plank flooring
that looks and feels like wood grain

and glue-down vinyl tiles
that you'd swear was Carerra marble
without the hardness, the coldness of stone

and it just makes me yearn for the real thing:

I want plastic to look like plastic again

that magic, elastic, neon bubblegum material of the future
of surfboards, urethane skateboard wheels and DEVO energy domes
of the flowing, undulating, impossible architecture of a Barbie doll

of a disposable shopping bag
discarded and windblown into the ocean
incandescent in the waves
like an angel headed homeward
to that heavenly vortex
where all the other
faithful, dutiful, discarded
plastic bags have gathered

Imagine Jesus back on Earth
in a polyester-spandex yoga outfit
— maybe one of those Lululemon hooded sweatshirt jobs
with the Yuppie Swastika on the hood —
an iPad tablet under his arm
and a pair of flip flops

made from recycled tires

No walking on water required

Just the miracle
of stepping out
onto this new polyethylene continent
soft underfoot
everlasting
and so easy to keep clean

I WALK TO THE BEACH WITH JENNA AFTER WATCHING *THIS CHANGES EVERYTHING*

by Wendy Morton

We find two sandals: a Nike, a Fila;
a Catchit, a green tennis ball, broken nets.
Styrofoam everywhere.
We load up: giant pieces washed in from China
or Japan, or tossed by a tanker crew. Fish food.
Fish death.
We find a broken frisbee,
a log boom raft dog,
a painted stone,
blue as hope.

COAL TRAINS

by Emily McGiffin

Nightly, coal trains
thrusting through the soft spruce
wake us with their couplings, crash

and grate that shake the house and jingle
stacks of china in the cupboards. They slide in
whistling, mile-long, bound for the swelling economies of Asia

from mines — Bear Run,
Deer Creek — you'd want to visit
for the wildlife-viewing if not

industrial prowess. Production at an all-time high
bends the Midwest flatland into growth curves
prowled by trucks that dwarf the average

suburban house. What riches from an old swamp.
One hundred forty-five billion short tons waiting
to hump into the daylight. Fifty thousand

square miles seamed with wealth, land lying ready
ready, crying out! for development, YES
to Jobs! Grow Trade and the Economy! Those natural

resources return tenfold in containers from China's
gay markets. Cosco and Seaspan fetch our toasters
and t-shirts, handbags, sofas, Nikes, while our marine

bulk handling plant — furnished with technology,
Best of Its Kind! — ramps up for this burgeoning flow
of affordable goods. Daily, progress

cuts a graceful arc along the North Pacific
shipping lanes, while the mines, the trains,
the factories, loading docks

keep up their good work 24/7. Even this
otherwise quiet backwater of the unindustrious,
this unhurried thoroughfare and happy depot

of the boons of developed and developing states,
plays its own small part: lubing the tracks
to speed the twenty-five million tonne throughput

on its one-way journey skyward. Now there's
something to get fired up about! The sheer
power in each car surging past to the far-off engine

pumping out SOx and good times: beach vacations,
GoreTex, all the little
party favours of the age.

Myth Explaining Some of the Crests (Chief Mountain's Version)

by Jordan Abel

"Myth explaining some of the crests (Chief Mountain's version). The ancestral myth of the Gitrhawn (Salmon-Eater) clan gives the following account: After the canoes of the people had travelled down the coast a long way from the North, they landed at a place called Ahlknebært, south of Stikine River. They were close Marhla'angyesawmks (now called Tongas Narrows). As the sockeye salmon were plentiful here they fished, caught some, and cooked them ashore. The day was warm. Gunas, a nephew of the chief, went into the salt water to swim. His fellows saw a large halibut come up and swallow him. They hunted around and watched, hoping to find traces of the fish. Soon they beheld the Eagle at the edge of the water, and close to it, the great Halibut. They caught the Halibut, cut it open, and found the remains of their kinsman inside. His flesh was already partly decayed, and he had a copper ring around his neck. The father of the dead Gunas stood at the head of the Halibut and started to cry: "This is the place of the Spirit Halibut." It became a dirge, to be remembered ever after. They burned the body and hastened on their journey south."

Marius Barbeau, Totem Poles, vol. 1 (1950), 52.

                    follow
              the coast

                 cut   open

              the dead
                place

the

    sockeye
       shore
the salt
      hunt

         the
         flesh
around

              the Spirit

                    the
              remains of
                    a
                  head

                                                        found
                                                    decayed,

account:

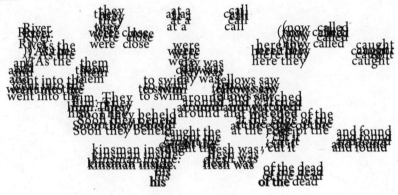

they   at a   call
River.   were close   at a   call   (now called   caught
)) As the   were close   were   here they called   caught
and As the   them   we lay was   fellows saw
went into the   them. They   to swim   clay was   fellows saw
went into the   him. They   to swim   around. Two watched
                Soon they beheld around and   at the edge of the
                Soon they beheld caught the   at the edge of the   and found
                kinsman inside.   caught the   cut it   and found
                kinsman inside.   flesh was   of the dead
                                  his   flesh was   of the dead
                                  his

the

                                plentiful
                    day

                                                    already

                                                                burned

HOLLAND AMERICA ·

by Miranda Pearson

Dawn: a peace-rose in bloom.
Day opens   pale, cold, perfect.

Sea charmed to stillness —
July by lotus-light.

Find a corner where they've forgotten
to install canned jazz and all

is the swish of the sea we move through,
the engine's low growl.

Porpoises nimbly   curl the air.

The tug and shift of ship, people scuttling
up and down, relentlessly social.

Multiplying, swimming, eating,
attending to our bodies.

We are animals, basic and social.
Moving through the strata of the boat, its

eleven layers of romance: promenade, stateroom,
observation deck, forward and aft.

~

On either side, blue-grey mountains slide by,
rocky heart-monitor horizons, stage-sets.

"Around 10 o'clock this evening we will arrive in Alaskan waters.
Wind your clock back by six minutes."

~

An elegant peak drifts into view, then behind.
The wake converged like train tracks.

Land's curve holds the memory of glacier,
it shifts like a sleeping animal, a hungry animal.

This is a world on its way to becoming
something else, a world remembering itself.

A dirty slope, forlorn chunks of ice
flecked with luminous eggshell blue.

Blue like a boy's eyes, and clear.
Toothpaste or chlorine blue. Pastel.

Vertical shards of ice, a close forest.
Ice with pointed ears, a witch's hat.

Ice of lacey spires, Gaudi-like
and not multiplying.

How fragile the glacier. Its wedges
clustered together like a frightened crowd

facing us, unarmed — we the strangers,
onlookers who cheer and click its collapse.

Ice porn.

The glacier leans in on itself
as if in consolation,

a grieving in blue and white,
the turquoise shards of Istanbul.

~

And the sea breathing, its throb and push.
Whales that wisely hide

from our human need to record,
to duplicate.

"Never think of this place as static,"
says the guide, through static.

Black-tipped seagulls flutter
over our khaki sludge that eddies.

Debris from the ship unravels into the water
its spooling thread inscribes,

casually paints
a future.

Rich

by Christine Lowther

for Jim Lynch

Cut the engine tie one rope to the dock drop everything
dive in clothes on best to purge it all wash the day's
drain from body and clothing
the water cold, so cold, changes everything

there are more things in the water than I might recall
a cougar, ears flat against her head, cruising islets
a black bear, one ear stapled orange, dog-paddling for shore
a diver glancing up, deer's legs thin-scissoring above him
       everybody's headed elsewhere

red-spiked sea cucumbers sprawled over boulders
dark multi-legged sea stars creeping like tarantulas
big sole flat tail-propelling undulations of grace
a trailing minnow-school its ladies-in-waiting

     a long-lost basking shark:
     harmless unharmed the giants drifted for millennia
     until men turned ships into blades
     slicing diligently
     they filled habitat with salmon farms
     drowned populations of sea lions
     there is more in the soup of the sea than I
     might fathom in my nightmares

Foot-long pale blue maze-striped mackerel circle sedately
stilt-walking kelp crabs cling double-jointed to eel grass
stone-carved camouflaged crescent gunnel curves over rock
one fish hurls itself *out*, a new definition of sky-diving
even now three seals are herding, scaring up schools in surges
I find myself among hundreds maybe thousands of fish

a blue whale couldn't squeeze into this bay
its heartbeat can be heard two miles away under water
its voice, a thousand miles
a child could crawl through its arteries;
if a baby right whale wants attention,
it will block the mother's blowhole to get it
more fills the untameable ocean
than I can summon in dreams

I can get out now. I'm me again. Peeling off
streaming clothes, towelling down,
I watch a merganser on a mission
a wind-up toy charging after some fleeing morsel
only to halt, lift her body like a lady's fine gown
and step daintily over my floathouse's taut rope

End every day this way
cut the engine tie one rope to the dock drop everything
dive in clothes on best to purge it all wash the day's
drain from body and clothing
the water cold, so cold, changes everything

AND I HAVE ALWAYS LIVED CLOSE TO THE SEA

by Onjana Yawnghwe

take your little earthquakes
and hide them away, ocean

my department catalogues pink shades
of salmon with round trip tickets

we have learned Latin to see
the names of seaweed

phytoplankton in green clouds
microscopes through kelp forests

we observe miniature galaxies
bioluminescent creatures in orbit

do the monsoons bother yet?

crevices drop
so mysterious
drop so
drop
so

the heart enlarges
and contracts
with the tides

when I thirst
I thirst for salt water

and I have always lived close to the sea

Break Gaze

by Shane Neilson

I've sat on pews and prayed a means
to intricate ceilings with the attention
due last things. To reach for what I need,
need has to change. The artefacts in our eyes
are offerings that form fantastical images
in the brain. Blueprints, secret plans,
survival methods of a broken artisan whose
eyes close on the broken things we unmake.
Remember when there were no wishes,
no dreams to come true, no stars, no Pacific Ocean.
Before we thought of dying every day? Feel a change,
a fathoming wide with hearts broken deep.
We cannot say its name.

The Living Infinite: Endangered

"It is clear that humans have become as powerful a geological force
as the four elements of water, air, earth and fire
that the ancients believed made up the cosmos.
Humans are so numerous, so ravenous, so self-centered
a species that we have become the fifth element."

— Alana Mitchell

GUTTING

by Joe Denham

Peel back the squirming tentacles
and slice the beak out like the stem
of a pumpkin. As I flip its head inside-
out, I can't help thinking *sentience*
of a four-year-old child, can escape
from a screwed-down mason jar, emotions
are displayed through shifting
skin colour. The dead, still-groping body
in my hands is dark, its sepia fluid
soaking into my sweater and gloves.
I bring the glinting blade down and
cut the blue-grey guts away, catch
my reflection in the steel-shaft
mirror: guilt-wracked, gut-sick
for two bucks a pound, fish feed,
tako sushi on Robson Street.

FALSE RIVER

by Bruce Cockburn

On the coastline
where the trees shine
in the unex-
pected rain
carcass of a tanker
In the centre
of a stain
and the waves of
dead sea things
slide slick on
to the stones
and the flux thick-
er than water
from the planet's
pierced bones.

In a jeweller's
armored window
You can just cast
your eyes on
a diamond-
crusted pendant
In the shape of
Bart Simpson
through mirrored
cops in armor
and the drift of
gas clouds
drones the
size of horse flies
scrutinizing
the crowds
and horsemen
on a high ridge
they wheel and

they ride
their work all
done for them
by the turgid
black tide

  False river
  dark flow
  How far do
  we have to go?
  Torrent tumbles
  to the sea
  This ain't the way it's
  supposed to be
  False river

Lifeblood
of the land
consort
of our earth
pulse to the
pull of moonrise
can you tally
what it's worth
We can spend it
till we end it
while the heat climbs
up the graph
till we're panting
like a salmon
with its gill hooked
on a gaff
and the dark blood
keeps flowing
like a hemorrhage
from the womb

that birthed us
gave us substance
On our own heads
be our doom

False river
dark flow
How far do
we have to go?
Torrent tumbles
to the sea
This ain't the way it's
supposed to be
False river

Herring Run (1)

by Cornelia Hoogland

1.

Because a bus
at high speed in white space.
Because a sky train. Freeway. Autobahn.

Traffic swells this poem —
tires over asphalt a kind of
whumping silence, the way we think
the Strait of Georgia is silent
when really it's roaring.

Or a barge. A container ship —
blistering furnace from China —
squeezes its hulk
through Seymour Narrows.
Cargo on its way to box stores.
On the deck sky-high cranes,
a dozen semi-trailers.
Blue polyprop rope.

Because a tiny deviation in the ship's
bank of diesel engines. The slightest
fraction of a degree
                off course —

            the steel hull shears Quadra Island's bedrock.

The only sound is waves, shocked
and leaping
high up Quadra's cliffs.

But under the water a decibel roar
takes off,
travels its warped, bent path —

2.

When sound hits the tympanic bone, the thin tympanic plate,
when the pressure levels (chronic at 202 dB re1μPa2s) accelerate
as tanker traffic and seismic surveys increase, when ocean basins
reverberate explosions detonated every ten seconds over
months, when shipping traffic doubles each decade,

it degrades the underwater acoustics, masks
the low-frequency whale speech,
interferes with echolocation
among the transient orcas
that migrate in late winter
through the southern end
of the Salish Sea for
the return of herring,
the Gulf Islands
thick with tankers
crowding the
already —
crowded
narrows.

The Memorial Service for Whales

by Kaneko Misuzu, translated by Yukari Meldrum and Alice Major

The service for whales is held in late spring
around the season when flying fish are caught at sea.

When the ringing of the bell from the temple on the shore
carries across the surface of the water,

when the village fishermen wear their good jackets
over kimonos, and hurry to the temple on the shore,

out at sea, a lonely whale child
listens to the ringing of the bell,

and cries — You are dead, mother, father,
I miss you, I miss you.

How far on the water's wide surface,
how far will the bell's echo go?

Pacific Ocean

by Brenda Hillman

{*a p'ansori* }

To feel emotion underneath emotion (a fertile dread
had mixed with ecstasy, not delight   such as delight

in nature   but of nature — a brew, a brink —;)

i went   to the ocean, my hydrogen host, was greeted in the negation
of the moment finding itself; put my hand to the surface & felt

the surface of emotion: a calm inside the prize, the gold halves

beyond the terms of argument   & terrifying acts of intent. When

first people sailed   in basket boats to never the place envisioning
an ideal, did the pelican   pass them   as here it passes —   its fine

head of z's?   Russian forts, frigates, a bit of fathom — Drake strides
onto land,   his sailors' lives handcuffed to expectation

(a borderous   dream is a dream —)

Everything i cried out & you embraced me: First threads of life,
paradise parasite — & have you heard   in juvenile gull-squeals (dent in

its beak) the deaf 'we are' braiding itself? Dulse, red algae, brown kelp

sizes us back … i cast myself before   the mind's trough — skin tent …

& the sun 'rose' a billion days in a saint's   circle of spikes …

Was aware of your west, volcanic aperture where flounder has no timing
was aware of your south; & suppose a flock   of beautiful ones wanted

neither to leave nor long — or … not wanted, exactly; between you
& it: amorous blood — (or so Agrippa writes of water's magic) —

The 'will'   before life's great cry — fear plus splendor, fame of joy,
internal skill to pause …   Carbon landed in no atmosphere;   plastic

(in the first sense) pre-eucaryote lineage — a trellis before
membranes (particular membranes … thicknesses —)

the sun rose a billion days   like the remorse of a bachelor.

Sea foam   condensed from early skins. i had a temporary joy —
We stand as a child in brenda's body   (thought forms — theosophy)

It is a long time   before they'll ruin you dumping phosphates

dumping degrees of plastic of   (of   of   of)   an I stands

kicking the foam,   coughing; there are   surnames   of stars in the salt …

When they stood here (or rather, environments. Environments
stood here) bacteria assembled before skins.   Rods, twitching stick-

shapes,   frenzied plates   or disks,   dismantling   minerals to hoard
fevers, in tenses — no duplicates at first sheen.   Steam stolen   from

volcanoes … Specific families are inside cabins, laughing, playing

flat games, laughing, waves lapping to this:

> *Great mother protect my mother*
> *Great ocean protect my father*
> *Great future protect the brothers*
> *& i saw a ring of stars in the water*

Copepods, jellyfishes allow   through   tunnels   of bodies
our laughter —   you are not "endangered" yet… One day   i will be

the word "fumerole" — pharoah yellow of same sun, the sex of touch —
(probably.   Probably touched.)   Red tide,   brown tide, young

young ocean.   Volcanoes called black smokers.   Deep hills' blind
forms breathed into   convolute curls of the mollusk (to which Benjamin

compared   a living room in Paris) — my heart closed   each time i felt
& when it opened   we were science.   Don't say lost.   Ocean, we

had been your   griot. Could you hear   backward? Pull
of the window shade, the waxen eye…

Emotions came   so late to earth;   hope passing through   the what…

Ocean has consonants, vowels & continents; it is a while   before
they'll ruin you …Life was found, as is commonly thought. The mat

of pre-cells puffed   & puffed. Puff-puff. Ha.

& the sun "rose"   a million days, like a proud nephew —

> Great mother protect the other
> Great ocean protect the otter
> Great godwit protect the godwit
> & i saw a ring of stars in the water.

Splendor, panic in awe, fear of envy, ragged   shame — propitiatory
dawns make emotions matter. Starfishes evolve: bath-mat bumps

on them, nucleic acids looking so Cyrillic, Urdu, Hangeul —
a cormorant stands by, in its 40s   movie detective trench-coat. Balm

to talk to you, ocean… Apophatic.   An ocean has   no   summary in tears.

Initiating curls of s~light change themselves   to pre-again, blue-green
algae   finds   carbon   for breath…   Names touch & leave: benthos,

nekton,   neuston, plankton — "eco-poetry"   families   of anemones
waiting for visitors,   pink nubbly prickles   defined

to wheel the gritty mollusks   in — (poets, save the names)

& the sun "rose" — Ahem,   like a civil servant …

You came so late to earth before life's great cry — Summer
in the spine,   types of tides (Neap tide, violet &   rare …)

Beige & other mists fall into footprints;   a thousand skinny

flies squint in my ear; it is a while   before they'll ruin you —

Removed my hat, my shoes. China's. Removed   China's shoes.
Socks. Removed   China's socks. Shirt from the Philippines,

hair thing from Korea; rings.   Europe's rings. Took off my
rings & walked   in — not to die … Baptists like to merge,

shamans like to fly. Through years, the bodies — near footprints,
moats, with brothers,   friends when i am not them;

otters' skins near Pt. Lobos — (almost wrote logos) in furry hecate
moonlight & further south where you take tiny raindrops to

Santa Monica's pier-legs coarse clingy beards holding mussels on —
Why were we 'life' & not nothing, she sang — clans & tribes

& the sun rises like a high school reunion, wise because past…

Methane to carbon.   Membranes assembled without air;   shreds
of light snagged   cynobacteria, plates,   circlets & disks,   nibblers

of sulfur, clans &   chimes.   We will name them   siphonophore,   for
whom "the crowd   is no veil,"   will name them   miracle, twin x's,

plover,   shark with   pursed vat-mouth, will call them   beer-can-
off- Stinson,   circumference,   sargassum weed,   radial gleam off

the Farallones ...why   were we this   & not nothing, she sang,

she might have sung ... i sang but i don't do beyond;
i do beside. Beside the ~~~~ ... & so on—

The tide is low &   safe;   water,   twin energy,   heard shell   shard .
scales,   plank & plankton   in minnows through   plastic six-pack
                        ooo
holder looks like   ooo   except for what happened is : it was endless —

The body turns   35, 8, 53, 81, 42 — it graduates to timeless & drinks
violins ... Beach flies around brown   kelp, brown   of beak   & burin,

sandpiper wild in sanderlings' syllable colony, shadows

like wine in a cave in Montara after the hurt joy ... It is while
they'll try to   ruin you ... Emotions learn to fold themselves

as does ∞infinity∞ : fin in it,   then in in   that, i in in,
energy & pure   annihilation merge in words, it said once; it   said that ...

(see spice routes, http://asiapacificuniverse.com/pkm/spiceroutes.htm)

what about specific 'maritime routes'? (i love the word 'maritime') —

First bacteria, rods   in their backs, disk-stems ... & then evolved
the forked gull- feet, then   love,   its beulah dream of awe ...

Century, come here   a minute & let's sing for the ocean:

Virginia, don't drown.
                        Gertrude, Mina, Hilda,
                        Marianne. Anna, Marina,
                        Elizabeth, Lorine, Muriel,
                        Gwendolyn, Cecília, Sylvia
                        don't drown. Denise. Barbara —

A verbed set of dolphins scallop on by toward San Diego. (Hi
Rae.) A cloud goes by, puff-, parallel to economics. Puff-puff.

Microcontinents   deeper than glades. Pelagic. Love   appears as
measure, a wreath of instances —

Great ocean protect the husband
                        Great future protect the daughter
                        Specific ocean protect the student
                        & i saw a ring of stars in the water

The tide was low &   safe. Lots of low laughing to draw emotion in —

Ocean, you exist as signs. Nature, you exist as   ocean. Everything,
you've become quite advanced   (for an everything) — Horizon strings,

nodes ...Quarry jewels.   Marine   squall squalling on up — golden colony
clumps. It is summer days   in California with jellyfish,   & in

the   mid-Pacific rift   where fish are blind, the giant squid

has writing in its eye, the   song has glass sides like a diatom —

& near the lighthouse orange lichen steps, pet apocalypse stars
fall down ... did did did did too, we saw them —

Countries, drop your countries.
Paraclete gull drop   signs in a ring. Poets, drop nothing;

you are asked to do the blind extraordinary thing —

the dream seminars go   on & on   beside which you are

the shaking figment — coiled life. Up & under & in —

THE SALISH SEA

by Anne Simpson

A tanker could be moving Savary Island southeast to Powell River.
Cliffs wobble, shift. The tanker passes, Savary remains, made of crushed

foil. History's trail of names: Bodega y Quadra, Perez, Galiano. Debris
of those expeditions, claims of wind over land. What happened
at Nootka Sound? Rain. Between the Spanish, the British,

a slick wash of grey blue. Three ships taken. The men's teeth loose
in gums, knowing they'd be dead long before

word came from the kings.

It rains; the ships go nowhere, sails furled. Between red cedars, women wait, sleep, wait. A girl works on a basket. Her sister untangles her hair with a wooden comb, two tines missing. One,

another

go down to the flats to dig clams, babies nodding on their backs. These ships have nothing to do with them.

Centuries tightly lashed — over, over, over — into a small cedar basket with a lid, topped with a square-woven knob, the right size for a hand, pattern of red-brown

on yellow. Morning tints the ocean, heat already lavish. June, sweet
water receding in the wells of the cottages. But still the motorboats, pleasure
craft, Seadoos, paddleboards. It doesn't matter

who won. Spanish, British. Smallpox

decimated the Nuu-chah-nulth. Look, what's left of the sailboat off Hernando,
a moth wing. And the cargo ship with recycled cars — trashed, squashed —
is an open jewel box. It glints.

A lost paddle drifts on the current, two logs, someone's orange lifejacket,
a couple of cormorants. Shadow eagles overhead. People could be lulled
by the warmth, balancing on sheeny rocks, stretched with seaweed emerald.
They could take each other's picture with their phones, a couple of selfies.
Nothing

after they leave to show
they were here. The tide remembers, forgets, remembers, forgets, remembers, forgets.

Vortex

by Alisa Gordaneer

Gyre[1] of nurdles[2] in waves, gimbaled ship-tipped waste[3]
jettisoned, lost at sea, dumped with invisibility wishes.

Microbead krill[4] sifts ashore, tropical turquoise stained-sands
bring paint-sample ocean to land. Damned, beautiful spot.[5]

Ingestion, starvation. Albatross bellies bloat fish-shaped[6]
Playtex shells,[7] lighters, bottle caps, toy soldiers and bears.

Bottled water bobs on water.[8] Fresh seeps into salt, we season deeper now.[9]
A tired sea turtle burps imitation jellyfish, discarded bags. Our clams self-preserve.

Debris field: constellations of perfect engineering,[10] discarded
conveyance. If nothing else, floating shrapnel bobs, its colours bright.

1. Transpacific gyre: Ocean currents carrying thousands of cubic metres of trash create what's known as the Great Pacific Garbage Patch.
2. Raw plastic beads, used in manufacturing. Estimated 250 billion pounds are shipped every year.
3. 33.6 million tons of plastic are discarded every year in the US alone.
4. An estimated 6 pounds of plastic for every pound of phytoplankton in an area as big as British Columbia.
5. The central cell of the Pacific gyre deposits plastic microbeads on Oahu's Waimanalo Beach, giving its sand a blue-green hue. Just south of here, tourists swim an endangered coral reef.
6. As documented by Seattle photographer Chris Jordan, in a series of haunting images of seabird corpses melted away from the piles of plastic in their gullets.
7. Childhood memory: pink, blue, white magic tubes found for beach sandcastles followed by rapid parental remonition and handwashing.
8. Every hour Americans use and discard 2.5 million plastic bottles, totaling 22 billion a year.
9. Researchers measured 250 particles of plastic per pound of seasalt.
10. United Nations Environmental Program estimates that the Pacific Garbage Patch has 46,000 floating pieces of plastic for every square mile of ocean, to a depth of 30 metres.

PARROTFISH

by Dan MacIsaac

Flamboyant bone grinder,
gleaming hermaphrodite,
bad wrasse hustler
at a funk stag fête.

Peacock party crasher
in kodachrome chainmail
and neon-streaked banners
outlandish and camp.

Sequined siege machine
at that bleak discothèque
of flood-lit plastics
and coral monuments

cankered by flux,
carbon-loaded seas
corroding towers
swarmed by debris.

O electric harlequin
shun hook and net,
dodge rupture
by toxin or blast.

O alchemist of rhinestones
rasp light from gristle,
moil bright sand
from riddled bone.

Note: Parrotfish chow down on coral, eating algae that would otherwise choke reefs already at risk from an acidic ocean. Coral ground and excreted forms the brilliant sand seen in Club Med ads. As they develop, these psychedelic fish shift colour and sometimes gender. Trans-fish in a Pride Parade, they have hip names: Queen, Green Humphead, Stareye and Stoplight. Overfishing is a major threat to the species and thus to the Pacific coral reefs and beaches sustained by the grazing of these wildly hued creatures.

AT THE AQUARIUM

by Joanna Lilley

Perhaps all the people streaming past
make Pacific herring think they're moving,
balled in a perpetual shoal
inside a lidded cylinder,
a giant jar of silver spinning fish.

Over children's heads and hands,
above the spikes of their voices,
I watch one herring flow contrarily,
nose up until it divides into purple bubbles,
a dark eye drifting out of its own light.

The whole shoal changes direction as I watch,
though I don't see it. I was observing
how only the back third of each fish moves.
There's plenty of space around this core of sea;
I still can't get past the sound of them.

You're showing me the five-hearted hagfish
down on the fake sea bed, sliding
into a dead fish's mouth and anus
like a turd pushing the wrong way,
to eat it from the inside.

You remind me to be thankful for the hagfish
and — your favourite — the Sexton beetle:
the waste disposer and the undertaker.
I look back at the herring trap, still hearing
the dizzy cram of the eternally shoaled.

A man and boy eat chips from a plastic tray
in front of the Quadra Island tank. In Australia,
two parents crouch to double phone-snap
their children glassed and laughing
at spitting whitebarred gobies.

In the Amazon rainforest
I grab the finger of a cecropia leaf.
At last there's no glass. I don't move
when water drips on my head.
A perfect ibis shadow tiptoes across the wall.

Sloths — dark burls above us — eat vegetables.
They take at least a week to digest a meal.
In the Strait of Georgia, the label back there said,
herrings' eggs are caught on blades of kelp and eaten.
When we leave, I avoid the jar of fish.

On the bus I hear them still, squashed
in that cylinder, sick with endless circling.
As soon as I'm in wifi range, I Google Pacific herrings.
It says they live in shoals all their lives.
All I'm hearing is water stirred in a glass.

Three Peninsulas

by Sijo Smith

I used to think that a crane,
long legged and
light feathered,
carried me over Beringia,
tracing the steps of ancient people.

That this flight —
filled by the roar of
an engine, not the rush of wind
through wings — was
my first glimpse of the
grey and blue
shattered-glass
mountains
and movement
below.

I'm on my third peninsula now,
always surrounded
by white-capped
and frigid
waves.

Even when I'm not
brave enough to dive in
feet-first,
the sea shares her song —

aware of
the vast solitude and
dizzying sway
of her salty curves,

the breezy scent and taste
filling our bodies; a balance

of reward and loss.

Here, the beaches are littered
with shells,
whereas at home,
Venus's clamshell would be
an ice floe
spotted with mud.

And for a moment I forget
the distance separating them,
delighting in the spray
until the mountain-top crumbles,

and I'm soaked with the drops
of upwelled waters,
their acidic chill
stinging my cheeks.

*"That sea star looks gross.
It's melting
like the Wicked Witch."*

And the sea butterflies,
fragile and pale, are as
imperiled as the Monarchs.

The waves impassively,
indomitably
carve the shores at our feet,
as we pull apart the threads —
unraveling the tapestry
and changing the picture,
inscrutably carving
away, upsetting
the balance.

A crane flies north
to witness a birth,
but Botticelli's shell has melted,
leaving streaks of mud.

My breath fogs in the cold;
a warmer release.
I alone am a drop,
but we are an ocean
bathed in moonlight —
the tug
of changing tides.

ONCE

by Anne Hopkinson

Once you see a glass sponge reef
you always see it,
fragile and strange, alive,
a structure like tubular vases made by drunken elves,
lopsided and droopy,
a world of animals fused together on a barren seabed.

Once you learn its story, you retell it,
its origins in Jurassic times,
its composition of spicules,
a rare and tenuous community of creatures,
filtering bacteria and plankton in ocean currents,
unique, an essential habitat
for rockfish, crabs, and shrimp.

Once you read the law, you doubt its strength.
Trawlers' weighted nets drag the bottom
and crush the reef in passing.
Drills swirl sediment
to choke and smother
a glass sponge reef.

Once you sail Hecate Strait, you love it,
calm seas at dawn, waves whipped by storms.
In Georgia Strait and Howe Sound
smaller reefs line the bottom.
Boat traffic churns above them,
anchors like wrecking balls hit the reef.
Count the ships, figure the damage.

Think of stewardship, of centuries,
our fragile contract with nature:
the only glass sponge reefs in the world.
You sign that petition, send that letter, stand
at the legislature, not once — once is not enough —
but again and again
until the law is strong,
until it is enforced.

Island View Beach, Endangered Species

by Susan Stenson

> *Far from the dream that is Eden*
> *it is hard for us now to believe* — Lorna Crozier

You'll hear them before you see them, she says. Points to
cocoons of water rollicking and returning to sea, dark shapes
on Canucks Jerseys and credit union signs, embossed in love letters.
Had a whale of a time. Love you more.

Trip Advisor's Number 1 on the what-to-do list: whale watching.
A skein of clouds crowds the vessel so sky is wool, sky is toque,
the heel of a sock needing mending between water and sky,
book opening, child pointing: water, water, water, Orcas!

Residents of J pod, feeding. Salmon skirting the ship, whales following.
Tourists shifting in their seats, mini-exorcists extracting KILLER
from the colloquial nickname. No context for near-death.
For WTF. For "… they pretty?" For WOW-KA-POW.

Esquimalt Lagoon, a Sunday, whale on the beach, a baby,
a black stone omen. Wind whipping sand, covering the bare
back in grit, a stymied funeral, no coffin; while in the distance,
a family flying kites in the shape of whales, cotton doppelgangers.

Whales learn what they know from their mothers, matriarchal
Akashic records, mamawhaleancestry.com. The whales do not
yet understand starvation, will not break the ancient codes, keep
idling the same waters during rush hour, ignoring foreclosure signs.

You should care about whale poo, the TEDx speaker exclaims.
Whales are ecosystem engineers stabilizing the oceans with feces
and rotting carcasses. Fecal blooms, a feast for phytoplankton.
Titanic prairie landscapes gather on water, burst into gloom.

The weight of a fifteen-pound brain roaming the Salish Sea.
They do not build roads. They have no maps. No picket fences.
Not one lawyer spins the strait. No crucifixions. No refugees.
No restaurants. No accountants assembling loss.

It Begins with an Image

by Betsy Warland

It begins with an image — toddler running to sea's open arms. Again and again, I have witnessed this instinct, this

— absence of fear —

Slosh in womb. Backward wave of toddlers, what changes when they finally turn it outward?

At 135 [degree symbol] W to 155 [degree symbol] W and 35 [degree symbol] N to 42 [degree symbol] N, the Great Pacific Garbage Patch held in the North Pacific Gyre.

Specifics of the Pacific: covers as much of earth as all combined land masses.

  — suspended microplastic particles, chemical slug, and other debris churn —

Water 71% of earth's surface, comprises 73% of our brains and hearts; 60 – 70% of our bodies.

Pebble and Montague Beach, Galiano Island; Southy Point, Salt Spring Island; Florencia Bay and Chesterman Beach, Long Beach; Jericho, Third Beach, and Whytecliff, Vancouver; Yellow Point Beach, Vancouver Island; Big Trib, Hornby Island; Cattle Point Beach, Victoria, sea homebodies to me.

The Great Pacific Garbage Patch contested/projected to be size of Texas up to twice the size of the United States.

Slosh of waves.

— unfathomable intimacy —

Caress of fields of grain-waves, sea far-far-away where I grew yet it surged in my Norwegian genes.

Long Beach, B.C. Summer holidays. Parking lot's solid line of vehicles facing Pacific. Predominance of prairie license plates whose occupants gulp horizon in again.

Yesterday: Third Beach, first summer swim. Inch by inch body temperature adjusts (our bodies keenly aware of each other). Fathom: feet leave ground. Every movement displaces, disperses, discomposes without rebuff

       — weight of saltwater (oh confident lover) strokes everything —

Oh Great Pacific Garbage Patch, countless marine mammals die in your abandoned, "ghost fishing net" arms.

ARISTOTLE'S LANTERN

by Lee Beavington

blackhole mouth bares sea-shorn teeth
midnight raises her five-fanged pyramids
her radial world balances the tide
as she churns kelp to weed and rock to sand
she keeps the seafood chained

without eyes the urchin holds the sea
perception starbursts beyond her calcite shell
a skeletal test for otters to best
consumes this ecosystem engineer
her mouth made for seaweed

she nurtures the nocturnal intertides
her roving dome an outward panopticon
perhaps this urchin is a philosopher
with senses no mammal possesses
in phase with every rippled wave

what did Aristotle see
when he was entranced by her spines?
that entrance to a geometric jaw
simple mechanics or a radiant threshold
window into the urchin universe

the only law she abides is natural law
a reciprocal rule we have forgotten
to her wisdom we are blind
if we held her lantern high
what question would she ask of us?

STILL FALLING

by Philip Kevin Paul

Below the burial ground, KENNES
has taken to its winter form, the echo
of its rhythm stumbling
into this ceremony of grief.

> KENNES is the name of the stream
> and the name of the whale
> that died in the mouth.
> I say the word and I can see the whale
> that beached itself there
> and the ancient man who found it,
> the fresh water of the stream
> falling around this enormous, slow-breathing creature,
> the whale feeling its own weight
> for the first time.
> I am standing with the man just briefly
> as he says, 'KENNES,' and looks into the waterfall,
> then at the whale
> washed up on the shore at low tide.

The winter has always been hard on us.

But when a family stands here together,
we know just what family is:
look how we hold on
to each other as we see
the casket sink into the ground,
my uncle's body
inside. Each of us holds a corner of this story,
though some of us have no hands
to speak of.

It's true,
when I feel helpless
I am the only one
who feels this grief.

> KENNES is the name
> of the stream and name of the whale
> that died in the mouth. I say
> the word and can see
> the whale that beached itself there
> and the ancient man who found it,
> the fresh water of the stream
> falling around this enormous, slow-
> breathing creature, the whale feeling
> its own weight
> for the first time.

How long had whales returned here
before this one? How long had people
come to witness their return?
To see them chase the young salmon
into the small bay,
nearly to the foot of the falls.

The body of a whale is like any body:
the canoe for an ancient spirit. The water,
like time, moving to the same edge on and on…

Still,
I feel as though I am witnessing
the first whale to wash ashore here.
My father's last living brother.

Uncle,
our last handshake in Saanich,
this shovel full of dark earth
on your grave.

TERENGGANU

by Kelly Shepherd

Pick one out from the shallow tub
of squirming and glistening
silent reptile movement.

Set it on the stainless steel plate.
Don't let it crawl off,
but don't exert any force:
both digital scale and
hatchling are fragile and sensitive
beyond what we normally imagine.

With the other hand,
copy its weight onto the chart.
Measure, count, check for symmetry.
Record everything.

Hold, between your thumb and two fingers,
this prehistoric beast:
its eye already on the horizon,
its tiny flippers already rhythmically churning
an ocean it has never seen.

Yesterday, you helped it out of the nest.
Elbow-deep in warm, damp sand.
Faint stink of snake;
careful fingers for soft eggshells,
clambering babies.

Tomorrow, you'll keep the crabs and birds away
while dozens of hatchlings leave the plastic tubs behind
and make their way to the open sea.
The gentle warmth, the undulating soft and green:
their mothers are out there, somewhere.
So are their deaths. Soon, for most of them.

164

You'll watch them scuttle,
funny and heartbreaking, across the sand.
Feel something you can't describe
when they first touch the water,
disappear into the surf:
when those squishy little flippers
actually begin to make sense.

The green turtles; the rocking foam sea.
In sun-warmed sand, they've been waiting for one another.
Two relentless surges.
These are deeper things, and older,
more powerful, than we can comprehend.

You could stand on the beach, and you want to,
all night. Trying to catch a last glimpse.
But the turtles are gone.
The ocean has them now.

And more nests are waiting,
more eggs might be hatching at this moment.
Tomorrow morning you'll start the process again.
Tonight, before you sleep, you'll pray.

VANISHING POINT

by Marlene Grand Maitre

She finds the last chinook, washed up
by the Salish Sea on Sombrio Beach,

carries the salmon home to ink its body, cover
in blue silk. As in *gyotaku*, her hands

trace its shape to lift prints, stroke
each scale and ridge. By nightfall,

a ghost school of chinook shimmers
on every wall.

         In home's uncharted depths,
she wakes underwater, pierced

by an orca call, a pulsebeat
of mourning, as the last

cow and calf glide
into the bedroom, drawn by hunger

to phantom salmon. At dawn,
both whales will wash up on China Beach.

She will wake 5,000 years ago,
on a Norwegian shoreline,

mesolithic woman, moved to carve
the first whales on rock.

gyotaku: traditional Japanese method of printing fish

Salmon Child's River Call

by Brian Brett

after Al Purdy

Sister, the waters
    are good,
the waters are salt and cold,
and the magnetic north humming.
The river is calling again.

The sun went down on the banks,
and we reached the kelp beds,
and then the big water
where the whales and seals,
the dolphins, sea lions, and tuna,
the flickering mackerels,
snapped around us —
all the lines and nets of the deep.
Sister, we have to swim for our lives
in the silver of our muscles.

Sister, I was the hunter, chasing
    the squid and the krill.
I ate the diatoms and the weeds
    and you the young grilse,
but I never took more than I needed.

I never took more than I needed.

Then I returned to the river, *Sister,*
against the current, past the wide delta
the wrecked shacks, the oil, the fumes,
the sour taste spilling out of the creeks.
Sister, this arsenical water is still our river,
the whiff of uranium and cyanide and PCBs,
this river is still ours, and we go glowing,
over the shallows, past the middens.

Call it the run of life,
never quiting.

Shining with muscle and desire
past the hairy paws of the bear
and the beak of the sudden eagle.
I am here… I am here…
in the spawning country of legend,
what's called the redds.
In the milt and looking towards
the rich colours
the evolutionary oblivion,
finning a territory in thé grave,
crisp with light and cool, cool water
where the shallows are clear
and the sun flashes golden through
the dappling alders and cedars.
Sister, where are you?
Sister…
Sister… ?
Where are you?

All the rivers are running….

CLOSE TO WONDER

by Kyeren Regehr

the elephant seal sheds her fur
down the road from my house

she'd hauled herself out
on Gonzales beach, *is it dead?*

still as the sea-worn
logs dragged to form a square

of tentative safety
mansions splendouring the shoreline

laminated pages of data and warnings
tacked to the wood

sea mammal undergoing catastrophic molt
please keep your distance. this sanctuary

further framed with strips of orange tape
lifting off the salty driftwood

flagging the breeze. an annual event
for a seal — a shedding

so radical she'll fast and doze
for almost a month
                              I kneel

in the sand by the barrier
you've got to get quiet

to see her belly blubber suspire
fur sloughing like old suede

or arbutus bark peeling back
patches of pink skin bubbled

and stinking like sun-warmed kelp
half-lidded eyes

        two teaspoons
        of crude oil

if I could get closer, and I won't
get closer, the ocean might

shimmer within
        a hundred years
        her kin hunted near extinction

      pups still tangling
      in gillnets each season

that smile curving permanently
under whiskered cheeks

she's a novelty drawing joggers
smoking teens, our word-of-mouth crowd

all afternoon. unguarded
from dogs off leash, kids waving

stiff wands of seaweed, tossing
trash to make her shift
        days pass

and when I think to visit, she's gone
two weeks early, her molt half-done

NORTHERN GATEWAY

by Lorna Crozier

Once there was a mourning song
a singer sang for four days
staring out to sea. That song is lost.
Everyone born here, every old one,
every spirit the salmon feeds,
every man inside a bear, inside a whale,
inside the throat of frog and eagle,
every woman whose chopped hair
tossed into the sea, grew into eel grass,
whose wrist and ankle bones
became the pebbles
waves rattle on the shore, every child
raised by wolves, by mother cedars,
by sea lions in undertows of grief —
these are the ones called upon
to sing a lamentation that will not cease.
You don't want to hear that song.

Slick

by Brian Campbell

Little slithery ink ball,
wings stuck.

Bleats from a bird throat.
Low slow moan.

Bodies lift, succumb
into gummy plumbed crude seep.

And the blot laps miles:
purple green sheen.

ANTI-LITANY

by Fiona Tinwei Lam

You should praise the mutilated world. — Adam Zagajewski

I've tried to praise the mutilated world,
those patches, shards and strands of nature
assembled and displayed into a dilute semblance
of wilderness. But all around,
the waves froth and foam, slick
with jettisoned fuel from busted freighters,
slathering all in a slime of liquid night.
Every day another discarded tonne
of plastic chokes and strangles.

I cannot praise our mutilated world.
Swathes of death scraped across the ocean floor.
Poisoned lakes. Amputated forests.
Murky skies thick from a billion
corporate exhalations.
Migrants' corpses beached
like discarded dolls. Swarming drones.
Remote control assassinations.

Who can praise this mutilated world?
What will be left on the other side
of barbed wire — those fragile, fading calls
of greenness, blueness before
they're trampled. That beauty
we remember, but
cannot resuscitate.

XCIV

by Sonnet L'Abbé

Earthquake. Say earthquake. Earthquake. A little shiver with the power to hurtle landmasses. Little wiggle of geological destruction. Oceanic earthquakes tremble down below; tidal motions, heaved by techtonic groan, surge; they do most damage to shores when waves behemoth. Moving motherfuckers, earthquakes. Earthquakes. Metaphors of selves as stone, unmoved, crack; even stoics get ruffled when hard ground torques like soft toffee. We tempt fate who live on the Island. Out West they rightly advise, on street signs: *here, tsunami threat* — above an innocent stick figure who races to higher land, the big wave curls … But it's the Island's nature to shudder; it's crisscrossed with seismic faults. Under oceans, moving expanses of mantle shift, rub continental shoulders; every day, imperceptible earthquakes flutter through roads and towns. North America is a plate of earth, stacked tectonically over Juan de Fuca, which pushes down beneath the Western coast. A subduction zone is what we're in, with Washington and Oregon. The Duwamish, the Hoh, figure thunderbirds — the Comox, Cowichan, Quileute, Tillamook, reference thunder-birds — the Yurok, Makah, Klallam, and Alsea stories refer also to water rising to the trees as Thunderbird (Eenumtla, say Yakama, says Kuykendall) once thrashed with Whale. The Huy-ay-aht, through stories, record the tsunami that leveled the First Nation at Anaktla, Pachena Bay. But believers of European data did not get why this subduction zone was so peaceful, until they started following up a forest extinction near Washington, then begot the Japanese an inferred seismic mom for their "orphan" tsunami. Earthquake. West Coast earthquake. "Myth" based in naturalist witness, centuries-old document borne in surviving narratives. Hupii! Looks like we're due for the Big One, sixty-five years overdue. A silent wave will set the dogs barking. Then things will turn shaky; houses will lurch, bridges twist, buildings fly off their foundations. Then the ocean, elevated, a five-storey wall, will swipe us right off the map. This Friday there's an emergency drill. We'll fearlessly review drop, cover and hold. The website teaches quake, tsunami, wildfire, and zombie preparedness.

WHAT HAVE YOU DONE FOR US LATELY?

by Dan Mangan

We are your prodigal son
We swam from your womb
We crawled the depths of the sea until it became the soil

We lit a fire
We tilled and we tilled
We choked on the air until our lungs accepted it

We ate what you gifted us
We built boats that became continents
We believed that you could give until we needed no more

We have raised hairs
We have barking dogs
We won't be settled until the kids come home

We return to you
We feel uneasy
We make predictions until until until

THE LAST STURGEON

by Steven Heighton

Deltawave shadows
of his deeds
and didn'ts, slid
under his shoes
like fillet knives, severing
soles from soil,
so he always walked
a little above his life,
not knowing it was
his life, while it waned
from waking-coma
to coma.
       Came a land-
locked night
he dreamed that he'd
landed the last sturgeon in the world
and she looked bad —
shrunken, bludgeoned,
a blue-ribbed CAT scan
of herself, her buckled
gills gawping,
a foam of green roe
welling from her mouth.

Each egg
was a tear, a tiny, entreating
vowel he couldn't quite hear
as he cast round the boat (now morphing
into a mountain shack)
for water, the merest
rainpool, he panicked,
or glacial stream,
my dearest,
my loved one,
let me bear you back
to haven — by river
the ocean
is never far.

OCEAN MEMORY

by Laurie D. Graham

The way the sky arrives on it, flat blue's far-off tongue, the height of the
sun's brightness before it, the Newfoundland novelist who doesn't get not
getting it, the way the funk sweeps through town like brewery wort, the
times of day the crows and gulls move to and away, the urge to seek a
vantage point, to sit above it, the climb down the rocks to be close to it on
a full moon, illicit and allowed, the corked wine bottles washing up every
so often, the trick-snake bull kelp and the slime an old relative, the way it
makes ritual, swimming a cold that imprints the core, people building
driftwood compounds beside it, the Surf Motel and its can openers, the
tourists on it, the gleaning, the dog shit and the joggers, the tankers and the
log traffic, the rise and the learning and the fear of it — still and looking
and looking and fearful — the crying beside it, the loneliness of it, the
separateness, the way it talks to you and the way you talk back, the way it
changes your cadence, your language, to know it's close, to see its seasons,
to hear it as you walk to school, to see it higher than the ground from afar,
the way the clouds come in on ukulele strings, slow and pink, to learn to
know you don't know it, to chart its rhythms, to eat from it, to sense the
plates beneath it, to hear its songs and the human songs for it, the way it
mists the air and the land, to learn stewardship, boats that have rowed for
tens of thousands of years, to pick through its pebbles and find glass
rubbed thin and smooth, and hard plastic, and how warm the air can get
above it, and how of the air you are.

Biographies

JORDAN ABEL is a Nisga'a writer from B.C. Currently, he is pursuing a PhD at Simon Fraser University, where his research concentrates on the intersection between Digital Humanities and Indigenous Literary Studies. Abel is the author of *Injun*, *Un/inhabited*, and *The Place of Scraps* (winner of the Dorothy Livesay Poetry Prize and finalist for the Gerald Lampert Memorial Award), all published by Talon Books.

MALEEA ACKER is the author of *Air-Proof Green* and *The Reflecting Pool* (Pedlar Press, 2009 & 2013, poetry), and *Gardens Aflame: Garry Oak Meadows of B.C.'s South Coast*, (New Star, 2012, nonfiction). She teaches writing and geography at Camosun College and the University of Victoria, where she is completing a PhD in Geopoetics. She is from Vancouver Island.

LUTHER ALLEN writes poems and designs buildings from Sumas Mountain, WA. He facilitates SpeakEasy, a community poetry reading series in Bellingham, and is co-editor of *Noisy Water*, a poetry anthology featuring 101 local poets. His collection of poems, *The View from Lummi Island*, can be found at othermindpress.wordpress.com

JOHN BARTON has published eleven books and seven chapbooks of poetry, including *For the Boy with the Eyes of the Virgin* (2012), *Polari* (2014) and *Reframing Paul Cadmus* (2016). Co-editor of *Seminal: The Anthology of Canada's Gay-Male Poets* (2007), he is editing *The Essential Douglas LePan* for Porcupine's Quill. He lives in Victoria, where he edits *The Malahat Review*.

LEE BEAVINGTON is a SSHRC scholar and PhD candidate in Philosophy of Education at SFU, and he uses poetry to teach science. He is also an author, photographer, and instructor for KPU's Amazon Field School, and he teaches Ecology, Genetics, and Advanced Cell Biology in the lab and field. Visit www.leebeavington.com

TIM BOWLING's twentieth book, *The Heavy Bear*, appeared in the spring of 2017 with Wolsak and Wynn. It's a novel in which the three main characters are the ghosts of Buster Keaton, Delmore Schwartz and a distressed fifty-year-old poet named Tim Bowling.

NICHOLAS BRADLEY lives in Victoria, B.C. *Rain Shadow*, a collection of poems, will be published by the University of Alberta Press in 2018.

KATE BRAID has written, co-written and co-edited fourteen books and chapbooks of nonfiction and prizewinning poetry, most recently, *In Fine Form 2: A Contemporary Look at Canadian Form Poetry*, co-edited with Sandy Shreve. A new poetry collection, *Elemental*, will be released by Caitlin Press in 2018. In 2015 she was awarded the Vancouver Mayor's Award for the Literary Arts for leadership in Vancouver's cultural community. See www.katebraid.com

TERRI BRANDMUELLER is a writer currently working on a book about family secrets and Internet genealogy. She holds an MA in Media Studies, and her poetry has appeared in various publications in the US, Canada and the UK, including *Barrow Street*, the *Toronto Quarterly* and *Ambit*. She lives in East Vancouver.

BRIAN BRETT is a poet, fictionist, memoir writer and journalist. His bestselling *Trauma Farm* won numerous prizes, including the Writers' Trust award for best Canadian nonfiction. *To Your Scattered Bodies Go* won the CBC poetry prize in 2011. A collection of poems, *The Wind River Variations* was released in 2014. The final book in his trilogy of memoirs, the award-winning *Tuco*, was published in 2015.

BRIAN CAMPBELL is a poet, editor and translator, based in Montreal. He is the author of three poetry collections, the latest of which is *Shimmer Report* (Ekstasis Editions, 2015). "Slick" was first published as a prose poem in *Passenger Flight* (Signature Editions, 2009). Visit his homepage at www.briancampbell.ca

TERRY ANN CARTER is the author of five poetry collections and five chapbooks of haiku. *A Crazy Man Thinks He's Ernest in Paris* (Black Moss Press, 2010) was shortlisted for the Archibald Lampman Award. Terry Ann has taught Japanese literary forms at Royal Roads University and is president of Haiku Canada. In 2017 she will serve a community fellowship at UVic in the Centre for Studies in Religion and Society.

Ottawa-born artist BRUCE COCKBURN has been honoured with twelve Juno Awards, an induction into the Canadian Music Hall of Fame, the Order of Canada and a Governor General's Performing Arts Award. He has always had a tough yet hopeful stance, to: "kick at the darkness till it bleeds daylight." In 2014 his memoir *Rumours of Glory* (Harper One) was released and this fall his latest album *Bone on Bone* was released, containing the poem "False River," written for this anthology.

STEPHEN COLLIS's many books of poetry include *The Commons* (Talon Books, 2008 & 2014), *On the Material* (Talon Books, 2010 — awarded the B.C. Book Prize for Poetry), *DECOMP* (with Jordan Scott — Coach House, 2013) and *Once in Blockadia* (Talon Books, 2016 — nominated for the George Ryga Award for Social Awareness in Literature).

MÉIRA COOK's most recent volume of poetry is *Monologue Dogs* (Brick Books), and her most recent novel is *Nightwatching* (HarperCollins Canada, 2015). Her latest novel, *Once More With Feeling*, will be published in the fall of 2017.

Most of the year LINDA CROSFIELD lives five mountain passes and an eight-hour drive from the Pacific but makes up for it by spending winters in Mexico. She's been published in *The Antigonish Review, Room of One's Own, The Minnesota Review* and in various chapbooks and anthologies.

LORNA CROZIER, whose latest book of poetry is *What the Soul Doesn't Want,* lives on Vancouver Island.

MAKYLA CURTIS is Scots-Pākehā. She is studying for an MA in English at the University of Auckland, alongside a Certificate of Languages in te reo Māori. She is a letterpress printer, poet and printmaker with an interest in languages and dialects, DIY publications (zines), and typography. www. makyla.wordpress.com

Author of five literary texts, SARAH DE LEEUW is an academic and activist working in the fields of medical humanities and colonial violence. Having grown up and spent most of her life in Northern B.C. (including Haida Gwaii and Terrace), she is an Associate Professor with UNBC's Northern Medical Program, the Faculty of Medicine at UBC.

JOE DENHAM is the author of a novel, *The Year of Broken Glass,* and four books of poetry. *Regeneration Machine* won the 2016 Canadian Authors Association Award for Poetry and was shortlisted for the 2016 Governor General's Literary Award for Poetry. His most recent book is *Landfall.*

GARY GEDDES has written and edited fifty books of poetry, fiction, drama, non-fiction, criticism, translation and anthologies and won a dozen national and international literary awards, including the Commonwealth Poetry Prize (Americas Region), the Lieutenant Governor's Award for Literary Excellence, and the Gabriela Mistral Prize. He lives on Thetis Island, B.C.

ALISA GORDANEER teaches writing at Vancouver Island and Royal Roads universities, and serves as the president of the Creative Nonfiction Collective Society. Her first book of poetry, *Still Hungry,* was published in 2015.

LAURIE D. GRAHAM hails from Sherwood Park, AB, and now lives in Kitchener, ON, where she is a writer, editor and the publisher of *Brick* magazine. Her first book of poetry, *Rove*, was nominated for the Gerald Lampert Memorial Award. Her second book, *Settler Education*, came out with McClelland & Stewart in the spring of 2016.

MARLENE GRAND MAITRE's poems have been published in a number of literary journals, one of which was longlisted for the *The Best Canadian Poetry in English, 2011*. Poems have also appeared in four anthologies, most recently in *I Found it at the Movies* (Guernica Editions, 2014). She won *Freefall Magazine's* 2013 poetry competition and the FBCW 2016 poetry prize.

HEIDI GRECO came west to the shores of the Pacific Ocean in 1970. Since then, she has learned to follow its moods and to appreciate them, whether stormy or calm. In spring of 2017 Caitlin Press published her *Flightpaths: The Lost Journals of Amelia Earhart*. Another collection, *Practical Anxiety*, is forthcoming from Inanna Publications in 2018.

CATHERINE GREENWOOD's first poetry collection, *The Pearl King and Other Poems* (Brick Books, 2004), inspired by the inventor of the cultured pearl, was a Kiriyama Prize Notable Book. *The Lost Letters* (Brick Books, 2013) includes a sequence of poems about Heloise and Abelard. Catherine lives in England with her husband, author Steve Noyes.

JAMELLA HAGEN's first collection of poetry, *Kerosene*, was published by Nightwood Editions in 2011. Her work has appeared in journals and anthologies across North America, including *Ice Floe*, *The Malahat Review*, and *The Best Canadian Poetry in English, 2010*. She lives in Whitehorse, YT, and teaches creative writing at Yukon College.

STEVEN HEIGHTON's most recent poetry collection, *The Waking Comes Late* (Anansi, 2016), received the 2016 Governor General's Award. His poems and short stories have appeared in *London Review of Books*, *Best American Poetry*, *Tin House*, *Poetry*, *TLR*, *Best American Mystery Stories*, *Zoetrope: All-Story* and five editions of *Best Canadian Poetry in English*. His most recent work of fiction is a novel, *The Nightingale Won't Let You Sleep* (Hamish Hamilton, 2017).

BRENDA HILLMAN is the author of nine collections of poetry, the most recent of which, *Seasonal Works with Letters on Fire* (Wesleyan, 2013), received the Griffin International Poetry Prize. She teaches at Saint Mary's College of California.

CORNELIA HOOGLAND's "Herring Run (1)" is from *Trailer Park Elegy* (Harbour Publishing, 2017), a book-length poem. Hoogland is the national winner of the 2017 *Freefall* poetry competition. *Woods Wolf Girl* (Wolsak and Wynn) was a finalist for the Relit 2011 National Poetry Award, the award for which *Crow* (Black Moss) was longlisted. *Sea Level* was shortlisted for the 2013 CBC Literary Awards. Cornelia directs *Poetry* Hornby Island* on the B.C. Gulf island where she lives. www.corneliahoogland.net

ANNE HOPKINSON is a Vancouver writer newly transplanted to Victoria. She writes poetry, fiction and memoir. Poems can be found in: *V6A, Writing from Vancouver's Downtown Eastside* (Arsenal Pulp Press), *Walk Myself Home* (Caitlin Press) and *Poet to Poet* (Guernica Press), and a number of chapbooks by Otter Press. She lives in Victoria, B.C.

MW JAEGGLE's previous work has appeared in *The Liar, ditch, The Claremont Review* and elsewhere. He splits his time between Vancouver (unceded Coast Salish territory) and Montreal (unceded Kanien'kehá:ka territory).

CYNTHIA WOODMAN KERKHAM has sailed the coastal waters of the Pacific Northwest for fifteen years. Her poems have won awards, including the Federation of B.C. Writers contest and The Malahat Review's Open Season Award and she was a finalist in the CBC's poetry prize. Her first book was *Good Holding Ground* (Palimpsest Press, 2011) and she co-edited *Poems from Planet Earth* (Leaf Press, 2012). She works as a writer and editor in Victoria, B.C.

BETH KOPE grew up in Alberta, lived in Quebec City and Australia, travelled Southeast Asia, China, Turkey and Europe, but now finds herself truly at home in Victoria, B.C. She has written two books: *Falling Season* (Leaf Press, 2010) and *Average Height of Flight* (Caitlin Press, 2015). She is currently working on a third book on adoption and identity.

SONNET L'ABBÉ is the author of *Killarnoe* and *A Strange Relief*. She was the 2014 guest editor of *The Best Canadian Poetry in English*, and she teaches creative writing and English at Vancouver Island University. "XCIV" is the ninety-fourth of the 154 poems of *Sonnet's Shakespeare*, an erasure-by-colonization that assimilates the text of each of Shakespeare's sonnets into 154 new prose poems.

ANITA LAHEY is the author of *The Mystery Shopping Cart: Essays on Poetry and Culture* (Palimpsest, 2013) and two Véhicule poetry collections: *Out to Dry in Cape Breton* (2006) and *Spinning Side Kick* (2011). She's assistant series editor for *The Best Canadian Poetry in English*. www.anitalahey.wordpress.com

FIONA TINWEI LAM has authored two poetry books and a children's book and edited *The Bright Well: Contemporary Canadian Poems about Facing Cancer*. Her work appears in over twenty-five anthologies, and her poetry videos have screened locally and internationally. She is a mentor and instructor at SFU Continuing Studies. www.fionalam.net

PATRICK LANE lives in Victoria, B.C., with the poet Lorna Crozier and their cats, Basho and Po Chu. He has published fiction and poetry over a career that spans more than half a century. His memoir, *There Is a Season,* published by McClelland & Stewart, has been in print since 2004. *The Collected Poems of Patrick Lane*, published by Harbour, was released in 2011. His new novel, *Deep River Night*, will be published by Random House in February 2018.

U.K.-born JOANNA LILLEY is the author of the short story collection *The Birthday Books* (Hagios Press, 2015) and the poetry collection *The Fleece Era* (Brick Books, 2014), which was nominated for the Fred Cogswell Award for Excellence in Poetry, and the poetry collection *If There Were Roads* (Turnstone Press, 2017).

CHRISTINE LOWTHER's latest book is *Born Out of This* (Caitlin Press, 2015), a memoir that was shortlisted for the Roderick Haig-Brown Regional Prize. She is also the author of three poetry books: *New Power, My Nature* and *Half-Blood Poems*. She lives in Clayoquot Sound on Vancouver Island.

TANIS MACDONALD is the author of three books of poetry: *holding ground* (finalist for Gerald Lampert Award), *Fortune* and *Rue the Day*. Her poems have been anthologized in *My Cruel Invention, Poems from Planet Earth, A/Cross Sections, In Fine Form 2* and *Best Canadian Poetry 2014*. She is a widely published personal essayist and literary reviewer and is Associate Professor at Wilfrid Laurier University in Waterloo, ON.

DAN MACISAAC's recent work was published in the U.K. poetry magazines *Magma* and *Agenda*. One of his poems was shortlisted for the 2015 Walrus Poetry Prize. Links to his verse in online journals can be found at www.danmacisaac.com. Brick Books will be publishing his debut collection in the fall of 2017.

ALICE MAJOR's eleventh poetry collection will be released in spring 2018. Her collaboration with Yukari Meldrum on translating Misuzu Kaneko's poems has been a wonderful opportunity to learn about a Japanese poet who is not widely known on this side of the Pacific.

DAN MANGAN is a two-time JUNO award winning and two-time Polaris Music Prize listed performer, songwriter and film composer. He lives in Vancouver with his wife and two sons. Mangan has toured extensively in North America, Europe and Australia and has released four studio LPs as well as a handful of other EPs.

EMILY MCGIFFIN is the author of two poetry collections, *Between Dusk and Night* (Brick Books, 2012) and *Subduction Zone* (Pedlar Press, 2014), which won the 2015 ASLE Environmental Creative Writing Book Award.

LORIN MEDLEY is a counsellor and writer from Comox, B.C. She has been published in *The Puritan, Portal,* and *The Island Word,* and was longlisted for the 2016 *Prism* International Poetry Contest. "A Bebop Incident in the Garry Oak Ecosystem" won the 2015 *Books Matter* poetry prize.

YUKARI MELDRUM is a certified translator and a multi-lingual poet who has published a book of translations and poems in anthologies as well as other publications. Alice Major, a former poet laureate for the city of Edmonton, and she have worked together on translations of a series of Misuzu's poems.

ISA MILMAN is a Victoria writer and visual artist. Each of her three books has won the Canadian Jewish Book Award for Poetry. She crossed the Atlantic Ocean as an infant refugee, to grow up in Boston. For twenty years she's lived on the shore of the Pacific.

KANEKO MISUZU (1903–1930) wrote 512 children's poems, not all of which were published during her lifetime, but her poems were rediscovered in 1983. Now they are loved by Japanese readers regardless of their age. Alice Major and Yukari Meldrum of Edmonton, AB, together have translated some of her poems.

WENDY MORTON has six books of poetry and a memoir. She is the founder of Canada's Random Acts of Poetry. In 2016 she was awarded the Meritorious Service Medal by the Governor General of Canada for her work with Indigenous youth and their Elders on *The Elder Project* and for *Random Acts of Poetry.*

EMILIA NIELSEN's debut poetry collection, *Surge Narrows* (Leaf Press, 2013), was a finalist for the League of Canadian Poets' Gerald Lampert Memorial Award. *Body Work*, her second book of poetry, will be published by Signature Editions in 2018. Currently, she is a Visiting Scholar at the Canadian Literature Centre at the University of Alberta.

SHANE NEILSON is a writer from New Brunswick. He published *Dysphoria*, a book of poems concerned with the abusive regulation of mentally ill persons, with The Porcupine's Quill this year. In 2018 he will publish a book of literary criticism on English language poetry from the Maritimes, also with The Porcupine's Quill. He won the Robin Blaser Award for a long work in 2015 and the *Arc* Poem of the Year award in 2013.

NANCY PAGH is the author of three collections of poetry, *Write Moves: A Creative Writing Guide & Anthology* (Broadview Press), and *At Home Afloat: Women on the Waters of the Pacific Northwest* (University of Calgary Press). She teaches at Western Washington University in Bellingham. More at www.nancypagh.com

ARLEEN PARÉ is a Victoria poet and novelist whose books include *Paper Trail, Leaving Now, Lake of Two Mountains, He Leaves His Face in the Funeral Car* and *The Girls with Stone Faces*. *Leaving Now* was listed as one of the annual All Lit Up Top Ten Books. Paré has been nominated for the Dorothy Livesay Poetry Prize, and she has won the Victoria Butler Book Prize, the CBC Bookie Prize and the Governor General's Award for Poetry.

JEREMY PATAKY's work has appeared in the *Colorado Review, Black Warrior Review, The Southeast Review, Cirque, Ice Floe,* and some anthologies, including *Make It True: Poetry from Cascadia*. His first book of poetry, *Overwinter*, was published by the University of Alaska Press. He splits his time between Anchorage and McCarthy, AK.

PHILIP KEVIN PAUL, a member of the W̱SÁNEĆ Nation from Vancouver Island's Saanich Peninsula, works with the University of Victoria to preserve SENCOTEN. He will publish his third book of poetry, *I'm Still Your Pitiful One,* in 2017.

MIRANDA PEARSON is the author of four collections of poetry: *Prime* (Beach Holme, 2001), *The Aviary* (2007), *Harbour* (2010) and *The Fire Extinguisher* (2015), all published by Oolichan Books. *Harbour* and *The Fire Extinguisher* were finalists for the Dorothy Livesay Prize. Miranda currently lives in Vancouver, where she teaches and edits poetry and works in Community Mental Health.

BARBARA PELMAN is a retired English teacher who divides her time between her home in Victoria and her family in Sweden. She has three books of poetry: *One Stone* (Ekstasis Editions, 2005), *Borrowed Rooms* (Ronsdale Press, 2008) and *Narrow Bridge* (Ronsdale Press, 2017) and a chapbook, *Aubade Amalfi* (Rubicon Press, 2016).

For the past seven years, DAVID PIMM has been working part-time in Vancouver. This down-shift has allowed him time to sing and write poetry more, both of which offer him far more enjoyment than employment (shhh!), which now no longer gets in his way.

KYEREN REGEHR's poetry has appeared in literary journals and anthologies in Canada, Australia and America. She has twice received grants from Canada Council for the Arts, and her first full-length manuscript is currently under consideration. Much of her childhood was spent shell-collecting on the shoreline of the Australian Pacific.

REBEKAH REMPEL studied creative writing at the University of Victoria. Her poems have appeared in the anthologies *Force Field: 77 Women Poets of British Columbia* (Mother Tongue Publishing, 2013) and *Unfurled: Collected Poetry from Northern B.C. Women* (Caitlin Press, 2010), as well as various journals, including *Contemporary Verse 2, Prairie Fire, Room Magazine* and *Lake*.

BRUCE RICE is a Regina poet and editor. Bruce has published five books of poetry, which have received the prestigious Canadian Authors Association Award for poetry and two Saskatchewan Book Awards. His most recent collection, *The Trouble With Beauty* (Coteau, 2014), asks if we can still write honestly about beauty in the land despite our footprints on it.

CLEA ROBERTS was born in North Vancouver and lives in Whitehorse, YT. Her debut collection of poems, *Here Is Where We Disembark* (Freehand Books, 2010), was a finalist for the Gerald Lampert Award and was published in German and Japanese. Clea's second collection, *Auguries*, was published by Brick Books in 2017.

JIM ROBERTS walks on the beach a lot. His first book was *From an argument I've taken with me* (Wolsak and Wynn, 2000). He is working on a book of travel poems and two sonnet collections. A chapbook, *Left Shoulder Voices*, was published by Frog Hollow in 2017.

RACHEL ROSE is the Poet Laureate of Vancouver. Her nonfiction book *The Dog Lover Unit: Lessons in Courage from the World's K9 Cops* is forthcoming from St. Martin's Press/Thomas Dunne Books in 2017. Also in 2017, Anvil will publish the Poet Laureate Legacy Project anthology *Sustenance: Writers from BC and Beyond on the Subject of Food*. www.rachelsprose.weebly.com

ALANA SAYERS is from the Hupacasath (Nuu-Chah-Nulth) and Alexander (Cree, Treaty 6) First Nations. She is a writer and PhD Candidate in the Department of English at the University of Victoria. Alana understands her world through poetry and loves to share her voice this way.

KELLY SHEPHERD has a Religious Studies MA from the University of Alberta, with a thesis on sacred geography, and a Creative Writing MFA from UBC Okanagan. *Shift*, his first full-length poetry collection, was published by Thistledown Press in 2016. Originally from Smithers B.C., Kelly currently lives and teaches in Edmonton.

MELANIE SIEBERT's first poetry collection, *Deepwater Vee* (McClelland & Stewart, 2010), was a finalist for Canada's Governor General's Literary Award. Melanie completed an MFA at the University of Victoria, where she received the Lieutenant Governor's Silver Medal for her master's thesis. She has worked as a wilderness guide on remote rivers in the Northwest Territories, Nunavut and Alaska.

BREN SIMMERS is the author of two books of poetry, *Hastings-Sunrise* (Nightwood, 2015) and *Night Gears* (Wolsak and Wynn, 2010). *Hastings-Sunrise* was a finalist for the 2015 City of Vancouver Book Award.

ANNE SIMPSON is a poet, novelist and essayist. Her second book of poetry, *Loop*, won the Griffin Poetry Prize. Her book of essays, *The Marram Grass: Poetry and Otherness*, concerns issues of poetry, philosophy and art. She has been a Writer-in-Residence at libraries and universities across the country.

The White Crow is CHRISTINE SMART's latest collection of poetry, published in 2013 by Hedgerow Press. Her first book, *Decked and Dancing*, won the Acorn-Plantos People's Poet Award in 2007. She is currently working on a novel. Christine is the artistic director for the Saltspring Poetry Open Mic.

SIJO SMITH is a rising junior at Stanford University. Born in Korea and raised in Alaska, he recently spent a quarter at Hopkins Marine Station in Monterey, CA, where he wrote this poem.

SUSAN STENSON's work has appeared in many Canadian literary magazines, most recently, *Fiddlehead, Geist* and *The Malahat Review* and on CBC radio. Winner of a Prime Minister's Award for Excellence in Teaching, Susan has been a proud faculty member of Sage Hill's Writing Colloquium, The Victoria School of Writing, St. Michael's University School and Camosun College.

ROB TAYLOR is the author of the poetry collections *"Oh Not So Great:" Poems from the Depression Project* (Leaf Press, 2017), *The News* (Gaspereau Press, 2016) and *The Other Side of Ourselves* (Cormorant Books, 2011). *The News* was a finalist for the 2017 Dorothy Livesay Prize. He is one of the coordinators of Vancouver's Dead Poets Reading Series. www.roblucastaylor.com

RUSSELL THORNTON is the author of six collections of poetry, most recently *The Hundred Lives* (Quattro Books, 2014), shortlisted for the Griffin Prize, and *Birds, Metals, Stones & Rain* (Harbour Publishing, 2013), shortlisted for the Governor General's Award, the Raymond Souster Award, and the Dorothy Livesay Poetry Prize. He lives in North Vancouver.

BARBARA TRAMONTE has been an associate professor in the School for Graduate Studies at the State University of New York Empire State College for many years. She was also a poet-in-the-schools in New York City and owned a children's book store in Brooklyn. Her poems and essays have been published in anthologies and literary journals. She has a chapbook of new poems coming out in the fall of 2017.

EMILY WALL is an Associate Professor of Creative Writing at the University of Alaska Southeast. She has been published in a number of literary journals in the US and Canada, most recently in *Prairie Schooner*. She has two books published with Salmon Poetry: *Liveaboard* (2012) and *Freshly Rooted* (2007). Emily lives and writes in Douglas, AK.

BETSY WARLAND, poet and creative nonfiction writer, has published twelve books. Her bestseller book of essays *Breathing the Page — Reading the Act of Writing* with Cormorant Books was published in 2010; *Oscar of Between: A Memoir of Identity and Ideas* with Caitlin Press in 2016. Warland received the City of Vancouver Mayor's Award for Literary Achievement in 2016.

GILLIAN WIGMORE's novel *Glory* is forthcoming from Invisible Press in fall 2017. She is the author of three books of poems, *soft geography* (Caitlin Press, 2007), winner of the 2008 ReLit Award, *Dirt of Ages* (Nightwood, 2012) and *Orient* (Brick Books, 2014), and a novella, *Grayling* (Mother Tongue Publishing, 2014). Her work has been published in magazines nationally and internationally, shortlisted for prizes and anthologized. She lives in Prince George, B.C.

ONJANA YAWNGHWE has been published in numerous anthologies and literary journals, and her first book, *Fragments, Desire,* was published with Oolichan Books in 2017. She works as a mental health nurse in Vancouver, B.C.

PATRICIA YOUNG was born in Victoria, B.C., where she still lives. Her most recent collection of poetry, *Short Takes on the Apocalypse,* was published with Biblioasis in 2016. A chapbook, *Consider the Paragliders,* is forthcoming with Baseline Press.

TERENCE YOUNG lives in Victoria, B.C., where he teaches English and creative writing at St. Michaels University School. His most recent book is a collection of short fiction, *The End of the Ice Age* (Biblioasis, 2010).

JOE ZUCCHIATTI spent countless childhood weekends fishing off the coasts of Kitimat and Prince Rupert, once catching an eighty-five-pound halibut when he weighed a mere seventy pounds. Now he lives cold and inland in Whitehorse, writes poems, rides skateboards and swims in the Pacific Ocean at every opportunity.

JAN ZWICKY's books include *Songs for Relinquishing the Earth, Forge* and *Wisdom & Metaphor.* Raised in west central Alberta, she now lives on Quadra Island. "Seeing" is from *The Long Walk,* published in 2016 by Oskana Poetry & Poetics, an imprint of the University of Regina Press.

Notes to Poems

Gillian Wigmore's poem "Brown Turban Snail" ends with a quote taken from www.montereybayaquarium.org/animals/AnimalList.aspx?h=Kelp+Forest

The following notes go with Russell Thornton's poem "The Young Ravens That Cry": Cherith Brook is where the prophet Elijah was fed by ravens (1 Kings 17). The black box containing the ball of light that illuminates the world, the old man's daughter as beautiful as hemlock fronds at sunrise — are elements of the Haida myth of the raven who steals the light.

The quote from Patrick Lane at the beginning of the *Humans on It* section is from the poem "Across the Strait Thin Clouds Whisper Above the Trees" from *Last Water Song*, Harbour Publishing, 2007.

The quote at the beginning of Kate Braid's poem comes from the poem "Milkweed" by E.G. Burrows.

The following notes go with Christine Lowther's poem "Rich": Canadian Fisheries organized the slaughter — by slicing in half — of four hundred basking sharks in fourteen years. See *Sharks of the Pacific Northwest*, De Maddalena, Preti & Polansky, Harbour Publishing, 2007.

Jim Lynch is the author of *The Highest Tide*.

The quote from Alana Mitchell on page 129 is from *Dancing at the Dead Sea* by Alana Mitchell, Key Porter Books Ltd., 2009.

Susan Stenson quotes from the poem "The Silence of Creation" by Lorna Crozier from her book *Whetstone* (McClelland and Stewart, 2005).

Acknowledgements

Some poems have been previously published in books or literary journals:

"What We Heard about the Sea" and "What the Sea Perhaps Heard" by Rachel Rose from *Song and Spectacle*, Harbour Publishing, 2012. www.harbourpublishing.com

Tim Bowling's "Found Poem of Strait of Georgia Insults" was published in *The Malahat Review* summer 2017 issue.

Patricia Young's poem "Mural" previously appears in *More Watery Still* (House of Anansi Press, 1993).

A version of Bruce Rice's "Origins" appeared in *Prairie Fire's* Anne Szumigalski issue.

Rebekah Rempel's "How I Envy Jellyfish" was previously published in *Contemporary Verse 2*, Vol. 38, Issue 4, spring 2016.

"Wolf" by Patrick Lane from *Go Leaving Strange*, Harbour Publishing, 2004. www. harbourpublishing.com

Gillian Wigmore's poem "Brown Turban Snail" previously appears in *Make it True: Poems from Cascadia*, Leaf Press, 2014.

Jamella Hagen's poem "Comparative Biology" previously appears in the winter 2017 issue of *Grain*.

Russell Thornton's "The Young Ravens That Cry" previously appears in *Birds, Metals, Stones & Rain*, Harbour Publishing, 2013.

Christine Smart's poem "Interface" previously appears in *The White Crow*, Hedgerow Press, 2013.

Clea Robert's "Swimming" previously appears in *Auguries*, Brick Books, 2017.

Jan Zwicky's poem "Seeing" previously appears in *The Long Walk*, Oskana Poetry & Poetics, an imprint of the University of Regina Press, 2016.

Catherine Greenwood's poem "The Sea Is Not Celibate" previously appears in *The Pearl King and Other Poems,* Brick Books, 2004.

Emily Wall's "Grace Harbour, Desolation Sound" previously appears in *Salamander* and in the collection *Liveaboard*, Salmon Poetry, 2012.

Emilia Nielsen's poem "Surge" previously appears in *Surge Narrows*, Leaf Press, 2013.

Beth Kope's "What could be more alluring than the tides" previously appears in *The Average Height of Flight*, Caitlin Press, 2015.

Barbara Pelman's "Tashlik " previously appears in *Narrow Bridge*, Ronsdale Press, fall 2017.

Emily McGiffin's "Coal Trains" previously appears in *Subduction Zone*, Pedlar Press, 2014.

Jordan Abel's poem previously appears in *The Place of Scraps*, Talon Books, 2013.

"Gutting" by Joe Denham from *Flux*, Nightwood Editions, 2003. www.nightwoodeditions.com

Cornelia Hoogland's poem "Herring Run (1)" previously appears in *Trailer Park Elegy*, Harbour Publishing, 2017.

Kaneko Misuzu's poem "The Memorial Service for Whales" has been translated by Yukari Meldrum and Alice Major. The original poem is from Kaneko Misuzu Doyo Zenshu and it was translated and is published under permission by JULA Publishing Bureau.

Brenda Hillman's "Pacific Ocean" previously appears in *Practical Water*, Wesleyan University Press, 2009.

Dan MacIsaac's poem "Parrotfish" previously appears in *Cries from the Ark*, Brick Books, 2017.

Joanna Lilley's "At the Aquarium" previously appears in *If There Were Roads*, Turnstone Press, 2017.

"Still Falling" by Phillip Kevin Paul from *Taking the Names Down from the Hill*, Nightwood Editions, 2003. www.nightwoodeditions.com

Kelly Shepherd's poem "Terengganu" previously appears in *The Bony World*, The Rasp and the Wine, Edmonton, 2010.

Lorna Crozier's "Northern Gateway" is an excerpt from *The Wild in You*, text by Lorna Crozier and photographs by Ian McAllister, 2015. Reprinted with permission from Greystone Books Ltd.

Brian Campbell's "Slick" previously appears as a prose poem in *Passenger Flight*, Signature Editions, 2009.

Steven Heighton's "The Last Sturgeon" previously appears in *The Waking Comes Late*, Anansi, 2016.

Huge thanks to Vici Johnstone at Caitlin Press for right away agreeing to publish *Refugium* when I approached her. Thank you Sharon Montgomery for the striking cover. Thanks also to Amy Reiswig and Barbara Pelman, my friends and helpers who got me through the pile of over 250 poems with their helpful notes and yes's and no's and also for their help with order and editing in later stages. Thanks to Adam Olsen for his introduction and stewardship. Thank you to visual artist Regan Rasmussen for collaborating with me to create artistic responses to poems in this book. I had a conversation with Larry Frisch in the spring of 2016 and he planted in me the word and concept of refugium, I thank him for that.

Thanks to friends John Barton, Cynthia Woodman Kerkham, Anita Lahey, Barbara Pelman, Patricia Young and Rupert Gadd for conversations on how to better care for this earth. Thanks and love always to my son, Colwyn Gadd, and my husband, Rupert.

Thanks to all the poets and publishers for writing new work and releasing these poems to this collection. Of course I understand that poetry cannot protect the ocean, but perhaps these poems can be the *Silent Spring* to release a flood of environmental awareness and action.

YVONNE BLOMER lives, works and plays on the traditional territories of the Songhees, Esquimalt and WSÁNEĆ nations. She is the City of Victoria's poet laureate and most recently published a travel memoir titled *Sugar Ride: Cycling from Hanoi to Kuala Lumpur* (Palimpsest Press, 2017) in addition to three collections of poetry, most recently *As if a Raven* (Palimpsest Press, 2014). For years Yvonne was the Artistic Director of Planet Earth Poetry, a weekly readings series in Victoria, B.C., out of which she co-edited *Poems for Planet Earth* (Leaf Press, 2012). Yvonne is deeply concerned for the environment and in every action and decision tries to consider her impact on the planet and its future.